Minka Kelly l

From Small Town to Hollywood Stardom

"Always appreciate the positive things in life and cherish the people around you."

Jodi Lynn Sommer

TABLE OF CONTENTS

INTRODUCTION

Albuquerque's low-slung stucco building squats along a frontage road off Interstate 25 alone, as if the adjacent fast-food restaurants and businesses are keeping a strategic distance. The Big Eye appears much more drab without the cover of darkness; the enormous leering eyeball and neon lettering spelling out ADULT VIDEO have worn out from the scorching southern heat.

The storefront is filled with adult toys, DVDs, and cubicles for watching porn. Peep show stages with individual booths are located on the back half of the structure, where patrons can watch live girls perform in exchange for tokens and tips. Similar peep shows can be seen in the Madonna video for "Open Your Heart," although they are a polished, sterilized version of this armpit. I have made up my mind, though. A coin-operated female can't have it that terrible, right?

Even though I've been working at Check 'n Go for minimum wage, it will take me months to save up enough money for a place of my own at this rate. In addition, my middle-aged supervisor keeps making advances. Last week when I declined his approaches, he dismissed me. I made the decision that using this peep show as my bailout will be effective. I'll have enough to leave in six months, I swear.

Three nights later, as I prepare to start my first shift and walk into the area of the building where the live action takes place, the smell hits me hard. It seems as though undiluted Clorox has been sprayed throughout the entire area. Every breath I take serves as a reminder of how filthy the Big Eye is thanks to the pollution. The industrial carpet is matted and bald, and the lighting is harsh. I've already washed my hands three times since arriving, and I make a commitment to never use the restroom again.

I laid my clothing on a chair to provide a barrier between my butt and the seat while getting dressed backstage in front of a vanity. I'm anxious but steadfast. I spill my lipstick and my hand trembles, but I quickly repair it before anyone sees.

As I wait for my first customer, I'm tense. A red light will turn on over my stage when he inserts a token, and the divider that hides me from view will raise. I need to be seductive and offer the client a taste of something soft he can't have because the only way I'll make money is if they slide a tip into my slot. We aren't compensated for appearing in the peep show.

Tina is making a loud, lewd moaning noise. Even at the front of the store, everyone can hear her. She is a skilled performer. I'll find out later that she performs using sex toys and plays with herself. It could have scared me away if I had discovered that on the first night, but I'm glad I didn't.
I recross my legs after wiping the sweat from my palms.

My red light turns on at last.
Let's begin! As I stand to dance, my heart beats against my ribs. I turn to confront a man who is sporting a dirty backward ball cap and what look to be undone pants as the partition rises. Everything about him, especially his unkempt, pale, and exhausted facial features, is more hyperreal than I had anticipated. I reasoned that since we would be farther apart, I might deceive myself into thinking he wasn't actually there. We both seem to be alone in the same room at this point. It's too personal. I consider leaving immediately.

He looks at me with anticipation, waiting for me to expose my body. He wants me to stir him on, to get him heated up to the point where he loses control, lets his dick out, and jerks off. The way this man stares, thinking I'm about to give him permission to give in to the impulse, will be with me for the rest of my life. I'm unsure on how to proceed.

I'm finally getting the hang of the moves. Even though I'm quite sure I'm not doing it correctly, I can feel a rhythm and can feel my hips moving. I turn to face him and walk over to his window to let him know I'm there. I'm prepared to become what he needs me to be, to let go of my sense of myself, and to demonstrate my physical prowess.

The partition between us smashes shut as I reach up to untie the knot holding my thin top in place and stretch my fingers into the knotted strands to loosen them. I'm overcome by relief. Thank God, I say! I'm not required to follow through. I've received a pardon.

Then regret hits me square in the face. He did not insert a further token. My first client is gone.

Tina's side of the room's noise level increases in the meantime. How many fictitious orgasms is she allowed?

I am awaiting another customer. I work hard and am tenacious. I can get the hang of this. However, my bulb is not lit.

Tina is counting a stack of money when I depart at midnight, donning a sweater and sweats. I haven't made any money.

Chapter 1:
Mom's Beloved "Bag Lady" Sketch

I have a special surprise in store for you, sweetheart. Mom bragged. She gripped her arms tightly to her chest as if she needed to stop the happiness from erupting throughout her entire body, as if it were an energy current that flowed through her and wasn't always within her control.

When I was seven, I frequently accompanied her to Crazy Girls on La Brea, which is a few streets from Hollywood's tourist district and hidden from view by half-acre billboards and colorful neon. Crazy Girls is located just south of Sunset Boulevard. I was eager to go since she wanted to show me her new act tonight. It was a welcome change from my typical routine, which involved being dropped off with neighbors or complete strangers and passing out on a couch until my mother arrived to pick me up well after midnight.

We were given a cheap offer to live in the storage area of an apartment complex where we once had our own unit by the landlady when Mom ran out of money to pay the rent. The 125-square-foot box had just enough space for her to move around, but as she shimmied and pranced around the space, her done-up, disheveled hair mirrored the Christmas lights she had strung up to make the space feel cozy. I smiled.

Maureen was adored by all and always brought the party with her. She addressed people as "sweetie" and "baby," inquired about them all separately as if they were her best friends, and gave them all of her undivided attention. She would make a point of complimenting your nose and you, especially if you didn't like your nose, for example. You felt as though you were the most important person in the world as a result of her warm attention, which was like a beam of light. Her genuine talent lay in this. Everyone was thrilled to see Mo, including customers, bartenders, dancers, janitors, and the DJ.

The backstage women were gorgeous. They jokingly referred to themselves as "girls" and gossiped. The room smelled of old cigarette smoke, whiskey that had been spilt, and Victoria's Secret lotion. However, they still gave off a strong, assured, and self-assured vibe. One would occasionally fumble back from her act and offer a long-stemmed crimson rose that she had received from a client. "For you, Mink," she would say.

I was also aware that Mom was unique among the other employees. Mom gave it her all and was the inspiration behind the acts while the others appeared pleased to show up and work their shifts. She created dance routines based on her preferred musicals, such as West Side Story, for the other women. She was beautiful, creative, and special in my opinion. I cherished her.

She was going to let me witness her do what she referred to as her "Bag Lady" sketch this evening for the first time.

The girls watched me while Mom prepared for her performance, and one of them led me to a spot where I could see the stage clearly while remaining hidden. I had observed Mom getting dressed and was aware of the trick she was planning. Disco lights in the main room multiplied the bright beams into an endless, swirling kaleidoscope as they reflected off the mirrored walls. Although it was almost ten o'clock and far past my bedtime, Crazy Girls was at its busiest that evening. By this time, the little throng had grown larger, and the floor began to shake to the rhythmic music with a powerful bass line. I hid behind the dancer who had led me there at the backstage entrance after feeling a surge.

A topless woman in a G-string performed an acrobatic turn around a gleaming pole on the main stage. A bag lady suddenly burst through the club's side door as if by accident, and I wondered how she managed to avoid being dizzy while moving in circles like that. She carried what appeared to be her only possessions in filthy sacks while wearing scarves, an overcoat, and multiple layers of sweaters. Her hair was tucked inside a knit cap that had been pulled low over a portion of her face.

Even though I knew my mother had timed my leave, it didn't matter. What will happen next was already known to me. She would soon be gyrating her hips in front of a complete stranger as the golden bra flew off. I had caught a few of the lap dancers in passing and noticed additional people roaming about the club topless. Even back then, I knew that Crazy Girls was a place where women stripped off for guys. Mom was attempting to shield me in her own way, and for a while I allowed her to believe she had succeeded.

At seven, I wasn't particularly proud of my mother's job, but I also wasn't particularly ashamed of it, mostly because I had no one to be ashamed in front of. I frequently stood alone among adults when I was with them outside of school.

My mother created a small blanket nest for me in a corner of the dressing area after her first performance since I was exhausted. As tiredness overcame me, I recalled the applause Mom's performance had received. I'd seen images of her when she was a showgirl in Vegas. She was very beautiful back then. However, that was before I became a single mom. Even though I was aware at the time that this club was a far cry from the glamorous life she had imagined, the guys had nevertheless praised and liked her performance. They had thrown cash at her feet. That was a success in a way, wasn't it?

The sliding glass door let in a torrent of sunlight that directly hit me in the eye. I had no idea where I was as I looked about. The apartment resembled a run-down motel room in its drabness and disrepair. My cheek was raw from sleeping on the rough, unpleasant couch. The shag carpet smelled like it had been inhabited by a cat that struggled to use the bathroom. Mom brought me here the night before.

I wanted to arrive on time because I enjoyed my education. I'm good at arithmetic and reading, according to my teacher. I loved playing tetherball during recess. But lately, I had almost always been late, and I felt ashamed of it. Timeliness was highly valued at the school.

Mom was smitten with these lanky, emaciated men. She had mentioned this person last night at the club, mentioning that he was from a rock band. She had warned me to keep my calm and that he was a good guy. I continued to look at him from the side.

I heard him calling a cab as I closed my rucksack and yanked at the Velcro on my sneakers in the living room. He showed up a short while later wearing faded jeans, a ripped T-shirt, and flip-flops. To lessen the shock of the bright morning light, he put on cool shades that were either prescribed by a doctor or purchased at a boutique rather than ones he just chose out of a bin at the convenience shop. He then grabbed his wallet. "Ready?"

He gave the driver instructions before resting his head against the back of the seat, as if it were too heavy for his neck, while the cab made a series of right turns through a section of Hollywood that I wasn't familiar with. I felt more at ease and confident that he was actually taking me to my school when we crossed La Brea and continued onto Fairfax, which was more familiar ground.

Josh's mother prepared him breakfast, looked over his assignments, and shared meals with him. They completed jigsaw puzzles and played board games. Although the landlady was also a single mother, their relationship was unique.

Mom brought me up after school that day in her chauffeur's attire—driving a limo was one of her side jobs—and I didn't realize I'd been holding my breath for hours out of concern that she may not arrive until she showed up. But even though she was frequently late, she always showed up, so I chide myself. The after-school staff was accustomed to waiting for her. Maybe I was too concerned.

To those she felt comfortable with, she was all touchy-feely and pleasant, chatting, and getting close. It was as if she had two distinct personalities. She hid herself, though, from those who may judge her. She was the schoolmate who was the most wary. However, when the lads in my class or their fathers caught a glimpse of her, they gaped in disbelief.

As a little child who was keenly aware of every change in her, I attempted to forecast her transition from a period of high to low atmospheric pressure. She had an edgy edge, and I could tell when she was being covert, as right now. It was my responsibility to control my own emotions and prevent her annoyance. She was erratic if she was under stress or, as she was now, worn out from too much partying. I have to exercise caution. Nearly anything may make her irrational.

When her wrath finally surfaced, it came on us both like a lightning-fast thunderstorm. Even if she didn't try to hurt me at the time, I had developed extremely acute emotional sensitivity to her moods. I needed her attention, so I asked her about the powder as a tactic. I hoped that she would see what she was doing and choose to value me over the drugs. But the powder always prevailed.

A janitor was emptying the trash as the club was almost about to close. The main room was empty. The other females had already gone. Mom's eyes were gleaming with prankish glitter. She didn't want the evening to end.

Mom liked to spend money when she had it, like she does now. Fast. She'd let me choose items I liked while she was in that mood. I rose after nodding.

I had woken up by the time we arrived at the Ralph's on Sunset, and we commandeered the empty supermarket as if it were a theme park only for us. She pushed the cart while I rode in it like I was on a Tilt-A-Whirl, squealing as she whipped me around the end caps and drawing mildly odd looks from the man mopping the floor and the high school students stocking the shelves. She was wearing short shorts that exposed half of her butt cheeks and a shortie, cut-off T-shirt. It required more than just my mother and I to garner significant notice in Hollywood at three in the morning.

Mom slept so deeply the following morning that I had to stoop down close to her face to check on her breathing. Her sweat had a putrid scent from the Opium perfume she'd worn the previous night, and her makeup had discolored the pillowcase. It was early on a Saturday. I wouldn't have to argue with her to get me to school, but I was left alone and idle.

We weren't really buddies, and Josh was a year younger. He would occasionally come over to play, but I had lots of friends at school. I didn't require more friends. I needed a full-time mother who didn't sleep through the best part of the day and cut the crusts off my sandwiches. Norma brought us four Oreos on a shining white dish after we finished our lunch. Everything seemed very cozy and idyllic.

Chapter 2:
How We Got Here

The Record Plant Recording Studios on Sycamore, just south of Santa Monica and east of La Brea, is where my parents first met in the fall of 1979. It is a plain-looking structure that might have passed for an accounting firm if it weren't for the hordes of long-haired musicians who carry guitars and basses through its halls day and night. Despite the fact that Bruce Springsteen, Tears for Fears, Chicago, REO Speedwagon, Heart, Whitesnake, Billy Idol, and Mötley Crüe performed at the studio in the late 1970s and early 1980s, it was Rod Stewart who was at the time the biggest name in music.

My father, Rick Dufay, was a French guitarist and songwriter with long, curly dark hair and a goatee. One evening, he and his producer and best friend, Jack Douglas, were in the studio working on a solo record. John Lennon and Yoko Ono, Patti Smith, Cheap Trick, and Aerosmith were among the musicians Jack was recognized for producing; he later became my godfather. Jack threw Rick out of the room as he became upset with how the project was coming together. He watched my mom slink by in a pink catsuit while he waited in the hallway while munching on peanuts. Her beauty astounded him, and he was eager to meet her.

Rick was going to see the fruits of all his labor as a musician, so soon he was packing to tour with Aerosmith. They weren't truly a committed relationship, and that's another factor. They simply got together and took each day as it came. Or, more specifically, night after night.

My mother drove the two hours to San Diego to consult her mother when she found out she was pregnant without telling Rick. My grandma Renee was the sun, moon, and stars to her, and I grew up hearing tales about her. They acted more like sisters than mother and daughter, spending all of their time together. Mom had worked as a showgirl in Las Vegas and a part-time model by this point. The rare callback where the producer only wanted to stare at her tits was all the success she had as an actor in her dreams. Her career was in a bind. She was similarly lost in life. Previously, she had three abortions. She didn't want to get pregnant again.

Mom informed Rick about the pregnancy and made a plan. She was adamant, despite his best efforts to persuade her otherwise by offering to pay for an abortion. The last thing he needed was to start a family. He was about to enter one of his life's most exciting phases. He had played in garage bands, composed countless songs, and picked the strings till his fingers bled for years in preparation for this day. His dreams would be ruined by fatherhood.

To help Mom start her new life, Rick drove to the closest bank branch and withdrew a few thousand dollars. Mom said Rick was out of the woods because she made the decision alone. With that, Rick got in his car and headed out, unsure of what he had just done but confident in his future. The next day, the tour's charter plane would depart for his once-in-a-lifetime vacation. He had no intention of missing it.

My mother cried as she showed me photos of her mother throughout my childhood. She occasionally yelled for her mother. "Mommy, I need you so much." With the passing of her mother, something inside her broke. I occasionally caught flashes of the vivacious, spirited young lady she once was and pondered her whereabouts. I never got a satisfactory response.

Mom needed to locate a source of security because her mother was dead and she didn't have a partner to help her raise the unborn child. Her past experiences had taught her that attractiveness and a man's protection are the keys to a woman's safety. She started looking for a donor. I'm not sure how she met David, but he ended up becoming The One.

When David's career was booming, Mom, David, and I shared homes in the Hollywood Hills, first in modest apartments, then in grand mansions. Their relationship was tumultuous throughout the whole of my upbringing, as if the song "With or Without You" by U2 had been used as a script. They split up and reconnected, got physical with one another, locked each other out of the house, and found themselves caught in a bizarre relationship from which neither could totally free themselves. I merely assumed that was how connections appeared.

In order to get away from David, Mom and I occasionally moved in with Claudia, Mom's best friend. Sometimes we walked back to meet him. David loved me adoringly and treated me as if I were his daughter, regardless of the nature of their relationship.

Rick had been playing with Aerosmith for almost four years, and the grind of the tours had worn him out. A few days later, Rick called Mom to make plans to meet me. At the time, Claudia was our roommate. I can't recall the meeting because I was so young, but Rick claimed that I was curled up on the bed out of shyness with a halo of hair surrounding me.

I grew to love Rick's tendency to act as the group's peacemaker and mediator, often acting against his own self-interest. Tyler was given the idea that Rick's predecessor Brad Whitford should rejoin the group. Knowing that Whitford's return would put an end to his own tenure with Aerosmith, Rick made the suggestion. He was accurate. When Whitford eventually made his comeback, Rick bowed out and stood back to see the rest of the performance.

Rick was then prepared for a peaceful life, and the timing was ideal. Rick relocated all of us to New York City because Mom and David had broken up, first to the Esplanade Hotel on the Upper West Side and later to Sneden's Landing, which is located over the Hudson from Tarrytown. We later relocated to the West Side near the park on 72nd Street. However, Rick quickly relapsed, and the two of them soon found themselves once more entangled in a web of narcotics and all-nighters.

One summer day, Mom and Claudia were enjoying a pool party and were fairly inebriated. Rick left for another location. The adults shared joints and joked poolside while I dozed off on a thin air mattress in the middle of the pool, relishing the splashes of water on my sun-warmed skin. I dozed off for a short while due to the motion of the water beneath me. The adults had all returned inside when I opened them, leaving only me and them.

Mom loved to share this tale because, in her eyes, it showed how much she cared about me and how far she would go to protect my wellbeing. She claims to have seen my floatie turned around when she peered out of the apartment window. She screamed and fled the apartment in a panic. She then leapt into the pool while still wearing her clothes and made her way from the shallow end to the deep end to pull me out. I sputtered as she dragged me onto the cement deck. She collapsed in tears and wailed over me when I began to breathe on my own, drawing the attention of everyone at the party. She never questioned why she had left me by myself in the water since I couldn't swim. Instead, she boasted that my almost drowning had done me no harm. After all, I had returned to the lake the following day, ever the brave little girl.

Mom and Rick's relationship was becoming more and more tense at this time. Most of the time, Mom was out partying, and Rick was restless. He had no idea what he was doing with his life or his work. Meanwhile, Mom was dating other men, leaving Claudia and Rick to take care of the children. Rick began to spiral.
When Rick called Mom out, my godfather Jack Douglas, who had been with Rick when he first met her, called the situation to a head.

After that, I barely gave Rick's absence a second thought. My mom was constantly surrounded by guys, and David in particular soon replaced him in her life. Although David was the one who raised me, I was aware that Rick was my biological father. Throughout my entire youth, David served as my "dad."

However, Rick continued to communicate with Mom over the years. About once a year, he would phone and ask if I wanted to speak with him. I always opted out. In David, I had my dad, at least in my eyes. Despite David's complexity, he was always there for us. Additionally, I found it offensive that Rick believed he could call anytime he wanted after leaving us.

Rick nevertheless kept calling to see how I was doing. The same was always Mom's response. She's in school, so she can't answer the phone right now, but she's doing wonderful, I assure you.

From his point of view, as Rick subsequently stated, "It was all bullshit."

Chapter 3:
Red Lobster

It's been like piecing together a jigsaw puzzle with half the parts missing when trying to piece together the events of my youth. I can make out a red barn in the left foreground, a pond in the middle distance, and storm clouds in the rear, but it's practically impossible to make out how these things fit together or define the border that separates them. To fill up the gaps, I've talked to Rick, my mother's friends, and the folks I knew when I was younger. Even still, the tale is put together using jump cuts and a jumbled timeline.

Psychologists have long held the view that people tend to remember their unpleasant experiences more so than their positive ones. Some contend that this instinct has evolutionary roots since it is more crucial to our survival to pay attention to the lion in the underbrush than the lovely birds chirping in the trees. It is also a result of evolution because our younger years tend to concentrate more on difficult memories. Younger people need to gather a lot of information since they have a long and uncertain future ahead of them, therefore they retain a lot of specifics about unpleasant experiences to assist them handle their uncertain futures.

There were undoubtedly moments when my mother and I encircled one another in happiness and love, when I laughed with Rick and revealed whatever small pleasure he gave me, and when my love for David gave me a sense of stability and tranquility. I can't see those times clearly, though, like those puzzle parts that are missing. The same red barn can be seen repeatedly. that lake. the exact same terrifying clouds.

Mom erupted when Norma, the landlord who had been allowing us to reside in her duplex's storage room, shoved open the large door to the two-car garage that fronted the back alley. It squeaked and groaned as she did so. We had entered the wood-sided garage that no one seemed to ever use through a side entrance off the backyard. This concept was created by Norma and Mom.

I wanted her to keep away from David for her own good. They merely accentuated each other's flaws. Nevertheless, I enjoyed his company. Being a father's child was pleasant. Even though there were times when I needed protection from him, he always made me feel safe and protected. Rick wasn't on my mind much anymore, and perhaps that was just a coping tactic. I lied to myself and told myself David was my father. That was adequate. I wasn't in need of Rick.

We had lived with Mom's best friend, Claudia, before we moved into the storage room and before our previous stay with David. I enjoyed that. Claudia actually made my breakfast and assisted with getting ready for school in the mornings.

One day I made a mistake or perhaps I was experimenting when I addressed Claudia as "Mommy." I didn't forget who my real mother was; I was only trying to win Claudia over. That way, maybe Claudia would take me in if something occurred and Mom couldn't manage to take care of me. I can now see that I had wanted to win her over with the use of the word "Dad"; David had always enjoyed it when I did so; but instead, Claudia appeared to have been smacked. As she knelt down to my level, her eyes flooded.

That Saturday afternoon, my mother and I moved our belongings and tried to make the old garage into a house. I brought a broom and knocked on every corner to check for scorpions or other critters that might bite me at night. We put up our tiny fridge and hot plate, together with a lamp, TV, and VCR, using an extension cord we ran from the storage room. In case it grew cold at night, Mom put additional blankets next to the bed. Before we finally purchased a rug, I put up my dresser in a space behind the bed we shared and made an effort to avoid treading on the oil stains on the concrete floor. Mom soon started to snore. After my eyes grew used to the darkness, I peered up at the rafters, picturing a swarm of spiders dropping by dozens of filaments and waiting to jump into Mom's mouth with her upcoming deep breath. Although Charlotte was a good spider, I wasn't sure the garage spiders would be as kind after reading Charlotte's Web in class. I finally went to sleep.

In that garage, we stayed up late watching movies and musicals while embracing in bed. Beetlejuice, Mary Poppins, and Charlie and the Chocolate Factory were among the films that appeared to be playing continuously. Our preferred activity was eating in bed while watching movies.

The day had been fantastic at school. Because there was always a schedule and order, and I knew what to expect, I loved being there. I was social. I excelled at sports and enjoyed playing tetherball and handball during recess, easily defeating any opponent who tried to oppose me. My teacher, Mrs. Sheridan, praised my intelligence as well. Assignments and tests have the numbers 97 and 98 on them, along with smiley faces in the margins. I took the front seat and listened intently to everything Mrs. Sheridan said. I would have been the happiest child alive if school had been the only thing in my life.

Mom and I had moved out of the garage and were once more residing in the Hollywood Hills with David, even though they were no longer a couple at the time. He probably continued to take us in because he loved me and felt bad for Mom. Additionally, she might be entertaining during a party, and God knows he likes to host them. Most evenings, there was music, drinking, dancing, laughing, and fighting until the small hours of the morning. I occasionally came across couples having sex.

These days, David had a new girlfriend named Charmaine, and Little David was also frequently around. He had my envy. When Little David was a little child, his mother left because she had grown tired of the way David treated her. He was older than I was, but he still visited because his mother wanted him to get along with his dad. David gave me more attention than he did him, and little David was envious of me for that. He desired his father's love, which I had.

I basically kept to myself and spent hours touring the Hollywood Hills when we were staying at David's. I would wander out in the thick undergrowth and scale the ridgelines and paths dividing Hollywood from the San Fernando Valley. I came across wild anise and honeysuckle, savoring the dark licorice flavor of the plant and savoring the delicacy of the honeysuckles. I would get lost and then be found, my cheeks and shins getting scraped, while making up tales of being an explorer.

I occasionally went to see my classmate who lived nearby. The man who developed New York Seltzer was her father, and they lived in a spectacular compound where he housed tigers and lions. I could sit and observe the enormous cats and other exotic creatures strolling along on tree branches since their house had been constructed around a three-story glass enclosure. She had my envy, too.

David didted on me, unlike the way he treated my mother. He drove me about to garage sales and swap meets in his old Cadillac, which I believe belonged to his father, and he bought me records and a portable record player. My most prized possession, a My Little Pony castle with a herd of My Little Ponies, was purchased by him. He always had Elton John playing when I woke up in the morning. He was a photographer, and the walls were filled with enormous photographs of recording artists, including an elephant-sized Billy Idol. David thought the world of me, and the warmth of his adoration made me feel important and taller.

After school, Mom and David would alternate picking me up, but Mom would frequently coerce friends into taking her place. She was constantly on the lookout for someone to take over her duties. David was always dependable.

Although the officers called to the school didn't use their siren to disturb the tranquility of the area, red and blue emergency lights were flashing across the school's front and the homes along Hayworth. I was a little bit excited. I had watched police pursuits on television and imagined what it would be like to drive a police car. I anticipated a journey. But then my intellectual side came to the fore. I ought to be scared.

Mom and David were always on the lookout for police, peeping through the shutters to make sure no narco investigator was keeping an eye on them. They had cause for concern. Both legal registration and insurance for their vehicles were never obtained. Drugs were frequently found in the glove box or behind the seat, along with warrants and expired licenses. David was suspected of dealing because the house had already been searched. I didn't want Mom or David to have any difficulties as a result of me tonight.

They drove me to the Red Lobster in West Hollywood in Santa Monica. We frequently ate at burger places, Del Taco, or Johnny Rockets when we went out to dinner. This was a step up, and although my stomach hurt, I wished I could appreciate it.

I made the fried shrimp my order when it was time to place it. I wanted to conceal, despite the authorities' repeated attempts to speak with me. I wanted to be somewhere else as I stared down at my lap. I was accustomed to my mother forgetting about me, so I had no reason to fear that she was harmed, missing, or would not return for me. Instead, I experienced absolute humiliation. I was ashamed that the police were having to watch me because I knew they had more important things to do with their time. The fact that I was a burden physically hurt me.

I knew David or my mother would find me eventually. I kept imagining the scenario in which one of them would appear. If it were David, he would be in his cowboy hat, grab me in his arms, and crack a joke about the situation. Then, things would return to normal. But for the time being, I had to let the evening unfold because I was in the spotlight. The officers paid the bill even though I hadn't eaten anything; they had nibbled on my fries to cheer me up and persuade me to eat. They then drove me to the station, where they started looking for my mother, and got me an ice cream cone at Fosters Freeze.

Unlike what I had seen on television, the station was different. I anticipated handcuffed individuals entering, radio activity, and perhaps officers glaring at me. It was much quieter, and I managed to drown out what little disturbance did exist. With the computer at my fingers, I entirely eliminated the sounds and fluorescent lighting of the station, content in my own thoughts. I had honed the ability to withdraw myself from practically any circumstance.

I worked on an acrostic poem, as I had been taught in school, using the letters of mommy as the beginning of each line when I got tired of entering my name. When she arrives, I'll tell her about it, which might make her feel better. She wasn't going to be pleased with this circumstance. The most excellent mommy ever

Before I could cross the room, the two officers dragged her away as I tumbled from the phone book in an attempt to get to her and bury myself in her arms. Mom was visibly yelling while waving frantically and pointing at me through the glass as they led her into a room with a glass wall from which I could see the three of them. Back at the computer, I repeatedly typed my name, believing that if I could get the letters to scroll smoothly and quickly—this time with no mistakes—I could convince them to let her go.

The Mercedes was waiting at the curb with a cool-looking guy in the driver's seat. She placed me in the backseat and gave the wheel to him. He had to be her "date" for the evening. She failed to introduce me because she was too preoccupied lecturing the other man about David's carelessness. She took the center console's brick-like vehicle phone and began keying in numbers.

Mom soon left David once more. This time, we moved in with a different friend of Mom's. As usual, we unexpectedly arrived at someone's door with our suitcases in tow.

The buddy would always unlock the door and let us in after Mom complained to them about how she couldn't possibly cope without their assistance.
I didn't like the pattern I was beginning to notice. It was exhausting to go from this friend's couch to this person's place, to a garage, and back to David's. My mother used to say that it was just the two of us up against the entire world. Together, we had the power to accomplish anything. But Mom wanted support from others, and I began to feel like she was dragging me along wherever she went.

Chapter 4:
It's a Jolly Rancher Life

Mom had stormed into the flat where we were staying a few weeks earlier, bursting like a volcano that couldn't resist erupting. She jiggled as usual in her little shorts that didn't cover her behind as she danced in a small circle while wearing thigh-high boots. Her halter-style yellow sequin top caught the afternoon sun, scattering sparks across the dark space. She waved a piece of paper like a flag while holding it high above her head. She would have been throwing confetti in all directions if she had had any. She hadn't looked this joyful in a very long time.

She held up the paper outlining the engagement's terms for me to see. I'm being dispatched to the Philippines! in support of a mobile lingerie exhibition. Claudia is also going. She'll perform some singing and modeling, but they want me to be the star of the show! Holy shit! Me!"

A while later, after leaving Hollywood's neon billboards and artsy mansions that talked themselves into the ridges of the hills behind, we were at the entrance of an apartment in the Valley. Now, all I could see was flatness. From the miles of concrete that built up the San Fernando Valley to the overhead power lines, smog had its dirty brown paw on everything. Here, it was hot. My T-shirt had become glued to my back during the car ride. We were standing at the front door when I tugged it to allow in some cooler air.

For the six weeks that Mom would be working with Claudia outside the country, Linette had promised to look after me. Did my mother pay Linette to house me? Was Linette a relative or a close friend? Nobody gave any justifications. I didn't want to stay with Linette, switch schools, or have Mom go, but I knew better than to voice my objections. I was unable to do anything that may dim Mom's happiness. Not now that she was getting out of bed and dressing by herself in the mornings. Finally, she started combing her hair and brushing her teeth. Even while listening to "Chuck E's in Love" by Rickie Lee Jones on the radio in the car, she sang along. She might continue to behave in this manner if I followed the plan.

I greeted Linette with a hesitant nod before she took me around the luxury apartment, which had a security gate outside, a marble foyer, and nice furniture. Amy, her 6-year-old daughter, wasn't at home yet but would be shortly. Every day, Amy's nanny picked her up and took her to school. Making a blanket bed on the floor next to Amy's canopied bed, I would share the lovely bedroom she had to herself. Maybe one day I'll have a bedroom that is special.

I was unaware of how fortunate I had it at Laurel Elementary, where I belonged and knew everyone. Though I had never been among the popular kids, I had finally settled in. I had no place being here. Everyone gave me weird looks. When I had money for lunch, I would walk to a stall in the restroom, close the door, and pull my legs up onto the toilet seat to make the room appear empty. I didn't want anyone to find out that I didn't have any lunch companions.

One day, classes were dismissed earlier than normal. The master bedroom door was open when I used the security code to enter the complex and let myself into the flat. A man's voice was audible to me. I walked to the kitchen to prepare a snack because I was used to coming home and seeing men Mom knew with. They soon began making sounds that indicated Linette wouldn't want me around.
I quietly closed the front door and waited just past the security gate. A short while afterwards, a man who was tucking his shirt in left Linette's flat. We exchanged looks as he walked away. Even though he was unaware that I was connected to Linette's flat, his gaze nevertheless gave me the creeps.

I was fairly intelligent for a fourth grader, or maybe nine-year-olds are smarter than we think. In any case, I got it straightened out. Due to the fact that she received her work while Amy and I were at school, Linette didn't have a regular place of employment.

As I was staying with Linette, David came and went from my life. When he was wealthy, he would appear and offer to take me shopping. He once brought me on a shopping excursion to The Limited. The garments appeared to be brand new and quite fancy. Then he vanished once more. He was a mythical, larger-than-life creature who appeared for a split second before disappearing.

One weekend, when the party atmosphere was at its peak, I was staying with him. He spent the entire night drinking, using drugs, and dancing with his buddies and his new girlfriend, Charmaine. I tried to go asleep after erecting the Care Bears tent David had bought me in the room with the least amount of noise.

The carpet was a mess this morning from last night, but I knew better than to start the vacuum and wake him up. For mornings exactly like today, he had instructed me to sweep the carpet rather than vacuum. I used short, swift motions to sweep backward while holding the broom at an angle so that the bristles dug in deeply. Although it seems useless, it performed a superb job of quietly cleaning the carpet and taking away any cause for him to be angry with me. When he occasionally woke up before I finished cleaning, I was in trouble. He would yell, striking me or grasping my face, "What is this mess?" At this age, he barely hurt me. He was still in love with me at the moment.

Gonzalez was David's actual last name, and he claimed to be of Apache Indian descent. When I was older, I overheard him debating his family history with his own mother. She corrected him when he said he was Native American.

A conga line of women waited to win David's favor since he had a way with women. It's not that he constantly courted them or showered them with affection, though he did both in the beginning of a relationship. David was a typical narcissist who preyed on women like Mom and others, making them especially susceptible. He helped Mom, who had low self-esteem, feel loved.

Now that I'm an adult, I can see how he repeated this pattern in all of his relationships. He would abruptly remove the charming mask after solidifying a woman's reliance on him. As long as a woman could endure him for that long, he would take everything she had to give— her kindness and nurturing, her love, her adoration, even her money. By this time, he had the women under his grip, and he complimented them on how fortunate they were to be with him. Usually, they had faith in him.

At the moment, Charmaine was his primary interest. Large, lovely lips and gorgeous, long hair. She was hilarious and spunky. I adored her earthy makeup, which included a brown lipstick with an opal shimmer. She always looked great in tight, high-waisted jeans. She was a favorite of mine.

At David's house, I was sound asleep when I heard an irregular banging sound that sounded somewhat like someone was hammering a nail but with less frequent thuds. I tried to fall back asleep after hearing David and Charmaine fighting earlier and calling each other names and using foul language. The banging increased in volume and intensity. To look, I stepped outside my tent.

When I entered the living room, Charmaine was pinned against the wall with her feet six inches off the ground because David was holding her by the throat. He was there in the dim light, looking eerily serene. Charmaine wore a brown suede jacket with fringes. They might have just returned from somewhere, or she might have been putting her jacket on to go. The fringe is what I recall most since it swung back and forth in a pattern that still gives me the willies.

The inside of my mouth had turned to cotton, and I wanted to scream, "Stop it!" I wanted to run over to him and yank his hands away from her, but if I did, I would draw his ire. I had to remain out of it for my own safety. I snuck back to my tent and covered my head with the pillow, feeling like a coward for not jumping to her aid. I had abandoned Charmaine, who had always been kind to me. He couldn't possibly kill her, I told myself as I attempted to fall asleep.

It didn't surprise me how violent this was. David always exuded a sense of danger, and he always made it plain that his viciousness was a menace. He made a show of having his chest out, as if to say, "I am the king and you will respect me." He once attacked one of his pals for using profanity in front of me. He said, "You don't speak that way in front of my daughter!"

I had previously witnessed him acting violently with other women, including my mother, before the incident with Charmaine. To be honest, Mom was also capable of dishing it out—to David and to her friends. She would kick, slap, punch, yank hair, and scratch. She occasionally cheated on me. I made breakfast with Charmaine the following morning. Her throat had bruises, and her eyes were puffy. She had a raspy voice when she spoke.

A few days later, Linette surprised me with a gift of Nike sneakers while I was visiting her again. I only had the cheap Payless knockoffs while the other kids at school got Nikes. She either witnessed me perusing magazine images or was able to read my thinking. She must have sensed that I was struggling at the new school and that wearing these sneakers with purple swooshes on a white leather base may help. I had the option to kiss her.

On my way to school every morning, I passed through a convenience store — not quite a 7-Eleven, but one of the neighborhood's many liquor stores — as I made my way to the bus stop. I visited the shop around once a week to buy a Coke or just to look around. I sneaked to the candy section when the cashier wasn't looking and threw a whole box of Jolly Ranchers into my bag. I was skilled at being stealthy and silent, as well as at making myself small to blend in and avoid drawing attention to myself.

I sold the candies to my classmates for a quarter each after I arrived at school. The preferred fruits were apples and watermelons. I quickly gained more of a following as "the girl with the candy" than as Minka Stinka. Together with my new purple swoosh Nikes, that made it easier for me to make friends.

I was sick of eating in the bathroom stall, and I had little interest in the cafeteria's food unless it was pizza. In addition, I detested the school's social order being established in the cafeteria, where everyone knew who got to dine with whom.

I bought two tacos on the way home from school using the money I made from selling Jolly Ranchers, and I ate them in the privacy of Taco Bell. No one there gave a damn who you were sitting next to. I was becoming self-reliant.

Chapter 5:
Here, There, and Everywhere

Because there was no order, only fragments of remembered events, and everything was jumbled in a chronology that I'm not even sure is accurate, the last two years of primary school don't unfold in my recollection in a logical sequence. I can now see that the coping skills I acquired to endure these situations helped me as a kid. However, as an adult, they have crashed into any buildings I have attempted to erect with potential life partners, causing cracks and fractures in the delicate web of trust I desire to develop. The old wrecking ball of taught habits keeps crashing into whatever I try to build, generating dust that sticks to my hair and irritates my eyes, shattering my efforts to smithereens even as I work to create a healthy and safe environment in which love and tenderness can flourish.

Mom abandoned me with these strangers because she had previously tried to care for me by relying on family, but it had not worked out well. She invited her sister Coleen in Oregon to keep me for a bit when I was around six years old. The conventional family structure in her home was something I appreciated, but it was very alien to me. Each night, the family sat down to have dinner together—how novel!—but it soon became clear that I hadn't yet been taught table etiquette. One evening, I disregarded the authorized serving spoon that was directly in front of me and scooped up a serving of peas from the communal bowl using my own spoon. I would have to eat the entire bowl of peas as punishment, Coleen determined in a fit of rage. The quantity of peas appeared to be huge. The only light in the home was a little lamb close by as I sat at that table until the early hours after everyone else had gone to bed. I couldn't leave the table until that dish of peas was finished. I spent almost the entire night finishing it. I have detested peas ever then. I haven't enjoyed them since a few years ago.

I was meant to be kept by David for a time before he came to get me. Linette shared the same outlook. She handed me a wonderful royal blue Adidas duffel so I wouldn't have to move with trash bags once more when she ordered me to pack my belongings that morning.

More than six weeks had passed since Mom's departure. I have no idea of her current location, expected return date, or current activities. Months had gone, that much I was certain of. My best guess was that she had been sent elsewhere after leaving the Philippines in search of new employment. Do you like stripping, lingerie shows, or the sort of bedroom work Linette performed? I didn't see why she had to be away from her profession for whatever reason, though. She ought to be with me right now.

She continued to check on me by calling, writing, and speaking with Linette on a regular basis. I replied as well. Our correspondence kept us in touch and showed me that she hadn't forgotten about me. She was the one who had informed me that I would be leaving Linette's today and staying with David until she returned. She had organized everything.

The afternoon hours went by without David showing up. When Linette picked up the phone, I was lying on my stomach in the living room, watching Chip 'n Dale: Rescue Rangers with Amy, Linette's daughter, sitting on my lower back and braiding my hair. My eardrums perked.

The same wave of embarrassment that I had experienced when the police took me to Red Lobster peaked inside. I detested being a weight on others. Since Linette was so sweet and this wasn't her fault, I didn't want her to witness my tears. I watched as Amy undid my braid and began a new one as I watched the two virtual chipmunks playing together on the screen. I did not shoo her away.

My throat constricted as a new blackness crept up my chest. Nobody was pursuing me. I had previously been abandoned because a plan's specifics had erroneously gone wrong. David or Mom didn't have their sh*t together, or their schedules didn't line up.
This was unique. I did it. They wouldn't pay attention to me because I wasn't significant enough, special enough, or good enough. This experience was completely new. There was a problem with me.

By the time I loaded my duffel bag into Isabel's Nissan Maxima, it was getting dark. Car headlights flashed by us like the strobe at Crazy Girls for a brief moment before the shadows engulfed our little group of people at the curb once more. I hugged Linette and Amy goodbye and held them closer than I should have because the Valley smelt like exhaust and recently poured tar. Although living with them wasn't ideal, we got along, and I enjoyed playing school with Amy.

For the first time, I understood how unique it was that Linette and Amy had embraced me and made me feel at home as we stood beneath the mercury vapor streetlights. Linette had a unique perspective on me since she understood how much of a difference a pair of Nikes would make in my life. And Amy was always genuinely happy to see me when I returned home from school. I was noticeable to Linette and Amy, unlike David and Mom, where I rarely felt like my presence mattered. As I said farewell, my lower lip quiver but I managed to keep my eyes dry. To avoid drawing attention, I covered my nose with my forearm while keeping an eye on my feet.

We took one of the narrow canyon roads as we made our way from the Valley to Hollywood, our bodies slamming into each other at every turn. I made an effort to remain subdued in my corner as

Serena and Marina playfully squashed each other. Serena worked to give me some room as Marina tried to shove her into me.

With braces, acne, and stringy hair that adhered to her face, Marina, who was fourteen and much taller and bigger than I was, appeared to be a seething monster. In my teens. Serena, her younger sister, carefully avoided Marina's rage as she watched from the corner of their bedroom, neatly tucked up in the closet. Bunk beds and white accents decorated their bedroom, which appeared to have been arranged for a television program. Was Marina upset that my belongings would ruin their dream bedroom? I didn't do it on purpose when her mother instructed me to place my bed next to their bunk. I also didn't want to be here.

My annoyance erupted in full force. Why did Mom leave for so long? Why didn't David pick me up? Why did Linette no longer desire me? I didn't want to switch schools once more, but I knew that was what was going to happen, and now I was trapped with this bully who was out to get me. I was so sick of having people tell me what to do, never having them ask me what I wanted, and always having to watch out for other people's feelings. What about my own?

Marina was thrown back by me, but I put up more of a fight this time. The fight continued, with punches, hair-pulling, wrestling, and rolling around on the carpet like two cats that had been tied together and put into a burlap sack. It was tiring to keep going when I was out of breath, but she was stronger and more adamant than I was. My breathing was ragged and rough by the time Marina sat on my chest and pinned me to the ground. Although it was a comfort to stop tumbling around, her weight was completely deflating me. My back and forearms were pricked by her fingernail scratches. My bruised shins throbbed.

This family's rules had been made very plain. I knew better than to call attention to myself, seek for assistance, or point out injustice, much like David in the Hills. No adult was coming to assist me, and if I told Isabel that Marina was a bully, I would only receive punishment. In addition, Marina made fun of me for sobbing. The sobbing had to cease, I realized at that point. I vowed never to cry again because doing so simply made the suffering worse. I had to keep my head down, try to blend in, and wait out the days till Mom came back.

Marina served as my jailer as a new routine was developed. She also kept Serena under control, and through our shared pain, Serena and I became close. Serena and I played Nintendo, made cinnamon toast in their gorgeous kitchen, and pummeled each other with her Koosh balls on the rare occasions Marina left us to visit a friend in the building. We skipped and laughed like people whose time is short and who want to laugh as much as they can before the jailer comes back and the door slams shut once more.

Marina repeatedly provoked me into a fight. We eventually ended up rolling on the floor, regardless of what I did or said. She would taunt me, and if I didn't answer, she would grab me and drag me into a fight. She attacked me right away if I spoke back. No one came out on top. The following day, in the shower, I would discover bruises and bloody stains all over my body.

During that long summer, Isabel was the only adult I knew, yet even if my life depended on it, I couldn't describe how she appeared. She simply vanished into the background, much like the instructor on Peanuts; her voice was the distant "waaa-waaa-waaa," completely unrelated to the plot. But Marina was a striking presence every day. She caused nightmares to keep me awake and brought on cold sweats. Even now, more than three decades later, I can still smell her, bitter and foul, a girl staking out her territory as a teen, warning me to stay away from her family, and defending her area.

When I returned to Los Angeles as a young adult ten years later, I was contacted on the street by middle-aged women I didn't know. They always embraced me tightly and were pleased to see me. Mom eventually came home, and to celebrate, she took me to Claire's to get my ears pierced. She determined that I was old enough for this milestone because I was now ten years old. I chose little cubic zirconia earrings.

Oddly enough, I definitely recall getting my ears pierced but not the day she really came back. Did I accompany someone to the airport to pick her up, or did she deliver chocolates to my door unexpectedly? One would assume that I would recall the scent of her shampoo, the firmness of her arms around me, and her surprise at how much I had changed. In the laser beam of her attention that day that was focused only on me, I bet I stood taller. However, there is a huge emptiness as if her return home never happened.

I suppose that by the time she did, I had cried for my mother too frequently, not knowing where she was or when I would see her again. It was just too painful, so I pushed myself to stop wanting her, waiting for her, and expecting her. She lied about her return date every time we spoke on the phone and was irksomely evasive about her whereabouts and activities. She should have told me, but she adamantly refused. I therefore blocked what I could.

Later, I discovered that she had been trafficking drugs for David at the time by driving a car across the border. She was apprehended and spent some time in jail, but she never told me. Years later, someone else gave me the details. Strangers taught me more about my mother than she ever did.

I recall being terrified of the piercing gun at Claire's, but its pain was nothing in comparison to the elegance and glitz of the earrings, which Mom claimed lit up my face. I took care of my piercings every night with a cotton ball and ear-care solution while admiring myself in the bathroom mirror and felt mature. While this was going on, I tucked away all the hurt and sadness I felt because Mom wasn't there and pretended it didn't exist. Instead, I concentrated on the fact that I was growing up and becoming a young lady.

Being in the hospital was almost enjoyable once the surgery was finished and most of the discomfort was gone. I was mesmerized by the tube that was draining the poison from my body via my tummy. The nurse told me how the tube operated since I wanted to assist her in changing the bandage. I considered myself to be a Frankenstein's monster since a row of staples marched across my right lower belly in place of stitches. The doctor allowed me to assist in removing the staples when the time came. In no way was being in the hospital traumatic. In contrast to my normal existence, when I frequently felt ignored, invisible, or like a burden, suddenly I felt cared for. As a result of the numerous Get Well Soon cards my school received, I no longer felt as distant from my peers. I marked a red line across the tummy of my Cabbage Patch doll, which I still owned, to make it appear as though she had undergone surgery. The original earrings I had lost were never found again, despite the nurse's assurances. My mother had to accompany me to get my ears pierced once more, and I chose the same studs.

We rang her doorbell again. You must have missed us, I know. Claudia was smothered in a bear hug while Mo sobbed. Claudia was shocked. She had not recently seen either of us. She had recently downsized to a one-bedroom apartment because she was now ready to live alone without any more roommates. Instead of Mom, Claudia once picked me up at the school gate. Her features appeared to have been removed, mixed up, and then reapplied in a peculiar manner on her face. She said, "Your mom is in the hospital. She'll spend a few days there. 72 hours, in actuality. It's only a minor infection, really. I hoped she would get some sleep. I didn't worry about her being there because my time in the hospital hadn't been too unpleasant. And indeed, she looked as good as new when she returned home a few days later after a wild night of partying.

Chapter 6:
A Fresh Start

My back hurt and my legs were sore from sitting for so long when I got out of the car to use the restroom and buy a Coke while Mom refilled the petrol. I exited the restroom at the back of the gas station and looked around. I-40 raced behind me, spitting pollution and fumes while being confined by a substandard chain-link fence. The sky above was dull and flat, as if the stratosphere had been covered with a Tupperware container. An abandoned planter next to the convenience store wall was filled with a jumble of sharp rocks, wayward tumbleweeds, and spiky cacti. Everything in Albuquerque appeared out of place, with every object covered in dust and every hue bleached by the harsh desert sun.

I was already pining for the greens of my hometown's vegetation, the rusty browns and straw-colored stretches of its hillsides, the shady glens I'd discovered in the Hollywood Hills, and the translucent blues of the Pacific when we drove to Venice Beach even though we hadn't even arrived there yet. With each inhale, Albuquerque's woe-begotten air filled my lungs. Fortunately, we were only visiting. or so I believed.

Mom walked back while carrying a bun on top of her head after paying the petrol cashier. Because it allowed me to view her beautiful face, I always enjoyed it when she had her hair up. Instead of having her typical seductive, messy bedhead, she appeared cleaner and more mom-like in that picture. As she made her way back to the car, the heat had made her brilliant green tank top look worn to the ribs. We were getting close after spending the entire night and much of the day traveling.

We traveled a long way in the mustard-brown car. Saab A few months ago, Mom purchased a used car lot. Before discovering the car lacked a reverse gear, she signed for it. The owner simply repeated the terms of the deal when she tried to get her money back. As is. Both Mom and Claudia had lifelong bruises on their shins as a result of being adept at shifting the car into neutral and pushing it into parking spaces. However, that was before Mom severed all ties with Claudia. Mom looked at the map and noted the location of David's family compound as I fastened my seatbelt. There, he was holding out for us. The only person we still had was him.

My first view, however, was quickly altered when David's parents—my grandparents—came out to welcome me. Speaking in a mixture of Spanish and English, they called to me, hugged me, looked at me, and showered me with affection as if I were the long-lost loved one they had been waiting years for. They bustled out of the home as if royalty had just arrived. Grandma smelled like rosewater and roasted chiles, whereas Grandpa smelled of freshly cut grass, turned dirt, and tobacco. Grandma arrived with an elaborate hairstyle piled into a sculpture on top of her head, while Grandpa, who was towering and had the moral authority of a giant, had hair that reached her legs. They seemed to know every detail about my past and were like characters from a book; they had all been there when I was born, even though I didn't actually know them. They praised my beauty and my mature stature as they petted me and reached out to touch my pale hair. There is no other way to put it; they were ecstatic about me, and I was so overwhelmed by their love and admiration that I didn't know what to do with myself.

They lived in a proper large ole house with numerous bedrooms that Grandpa had built himself instead of the small and dark apartment we had shared in Hollywood, which equally astounded me as their devotion to me did. I observed that everything had a tendency to roll as they toured me about because the walls were all listed, the doors gapped, and the floors were inclined. The fact that everything was haphazard didn't bother me in the least. The bedrooms of the jerry-built home were each adorned in a distinct hue and given a color name. I was overjoyed when Grandma allocated Mom and me to the Pink Room. Albuquerque gave me a sense of homecoming.

Due to the fact that Roseanne, David's elder sister, had returned home in the latter stages of AIDS, Mom and I had traveled to Albuquerque to be there for David. This property had served as a home for David and his siblings at various points in their lives. Because it was where they felt most comfortable, Roseanne wanted to pass away there. Lisa, Vickie, and Lisanne were the three girls that Roseanne was the mother of. I was protected from the worst of her illness by David and my mother. Although I didn't know much about AIDS, I was aware that I couldn't contract it by embracing or holding hands with someone, so I didn't avoid Roseanne. For the brief time we were together, I tried to be a kind niece.

After Roseanne died away, her daughters experienced the same warmth and love from the family as I had. That was how our family operated—it took in wandering souls in search of a place to call home, embraced everyone into its warm domestic embrace, and made room for everyone. I quickly assimilated into the compound's daily routine, picking up new ways of being and interacting.

Nothing in Grandpa's church, which was off a dirt road, was up to code; it was a simple square room with a lot of benches and a podium at the front. The walls, ceiling, and floors were also uneven. The pastel-blue and white imitation floral arrangements were illuminated by fluorescent lighting, deflecting attention from the low ceiling and dirt-brown low pile carpet. I didn't enjoy traveling with Grandma since I didn't understand much, but I did enjoy being taken care of and feeling wanted and loved by her because Grandpa served a Spanish-speaking church. Grandmothering was fun for me. I never did master Spanish during my time in Albuquerque and occasionally dozed off on her shoulder during worship. She would pinch my leg to wake me up if that happened. I retorted, "But I don't understand what he's saying."

The Church occasionally stunned or surprised me. Wailing and screaming could always be heard throughout the building, usually coming from the congregation's female members. Their hands were always extended toward God, Jesus, and possibly even my grandfather, pleading and requesting assistance. As they prayed, I could feel their anguish and knew it was genuine. The pain they felt was distinct from Mom's. Sometimes I thought that everything would work out for Mom and for us if she could just get her act together, do the right thing, and get out of her own way. She had a few options.

Furthermore, religion conveyed conflicting ideas. Grandma occasionally claimed that because I wore jeans, cut my hair, and eventually used makeup, I was going to hell. She occasionally said, "You're an embarrassment to your grandfather and the church," but I never took it personally. I was aware that my grandfather loved me dearly and always rejoiced to see me. Grandma simply had a strong commitment to her faith. Grandma tore off the cross from my cousin's necklace as she entered the house wearing it. Would you wear a gun around your neck if a gun killed your husband? Grandma's strict religious beliefs were downplayed by everyone, and I found comfort in how much she loved us. She always referred to me as Mija, which was so comforting, and she gave me responsibilities in the kitchen and taught me how to cook tortillas, which helped me feel at home. I belonged to the family.

Despite Grandma's dogmatism, I trusted her acts and thought they spoke the truth since deeds spoke louder than words. Grandma and Grandpa's house was a place of hope for me, just as the church was for many people in that working-class immigrant neighborhood.
Mom began working as a dancer at a neighborhood club that summer, leaving each night to go to work and returning to sleep throughout the day. My grandparents never judged or asked too many probing questions; they just wanted us all to be together. I think they were either unaware of her line of work or in denial. Similar to L.A., Mom was frequently conspicuously absent from this large family's daily activities. Karlotta, David's then-girlfriend, and I occasionally developed a mother-daughter bond that made me feel appreciated, like helping out with the family's tamale business.

The family of David earned a living in a number of ways. David was a fantastic cook, and the next year he launched his own catering company for tamales. However, that first summer, the entire family participated in the tamale-making process. David oversaw the production line as Grandma cared for the meat, masa, and chile sauces on a separate stove.

We arrived at construction sites early in the morning, at lunchtime, and in the late afternoon when the work teams finished for the day, peddling our wares out of the trunk. These were the times when I felt a part of this larger family and appreciated having Karlotta around as a sort of fictitious mother.

I still don't know if staying in Albuquerque was always her intention. I enjoyed the notion that perhaps she was altering her original plan only to fit my newly discovered joy, but the reality is probably more abrasive. In Los Angeles, we truly lacked a place to return to. In any case, I was totally on board when she offered that we stay and start a new life in New Mexico.

I was quickly enrolled at Taft Middle School by my mother, and if I thought I was isolated in Los Angeles, that was nothing compared to what I encountered there. The school was located in an area of Albuquerque where all of the residents were Mexican or Native Americans. I assumed that because I was so accustomed to fitting in with my vast extended family at home, I could do the same at school. I was oblivious to how odd-looking I was as a small, blond girl from Los Angeles.

After my first day at my new school, which had adult lockers and separate classes for each period, a group of girls followed me as I made my way home. They had been giving me unsavory looks at school all day, but I had no idea why. I attempted to keep to myself while sporting tomboyish, baggy skater attire. Why did they have it out for me?

My cousin came out of the yard at that precise moment to greet me. Yaz was sixteen, a little overweight, had thick, curling black hair, bangs that were fanning out, and wore a lot of cosmetics. She was the chola you wanted to stay away from. She socialized with the 18th Street Gang and made it known to everyone that she was a member of them. Although I would have been afraid of her if she weren't my cousin, her frightening presence was just what I needed at this moment to send these females a strong message.

Yasmn, who resided in the property with her parents and brother Rob, was Auntie Loretta's little daughter. She and our cousin Lisa were where I spent the majority of my leisure time. Lisa was fifteen years old, had long, straight, beautiful black hair, and was stunning in her own skin without any makeup. She was the family's decent child and the one who adhered to religion, taking Grandpa and Grandma's teachings to heart. while her mother passed away while she was so young, her faith provided her with solace.

Yasmn determined that I needed to improve not only my bad fashion sense—I needed to stop dressing like a crazy skater girl from L.A. and start wearing like a local—but also my lack of fighting skills. The day I saw Marina in the rearview mirror for the last time, I believed I had left all the strife in Los Angeles behind. I told Yaz that learning to fight was the last thing I wanted to do.

Yasmn recited the first few verses of a song by LL Cool J. I sang along because I recognized the lyrics. We were two young girls singing together about being by themselves in a room, staring at a wall, and realizing for the first time that "I need love."

Yasmin's parents were both addicts, so her family situation wasn't much better than mine. My aunt Loretta, who was her mother, had spent years going in and out of rehab and was now covered in scabs from head to toe. Yasmin once discovered her parents dozing off on the couch with a needle poking out of her father's arm while I was with her in her back unit. After that, David stopped letting me go see them. I knew it was horrible if even David wouldn't let me leave.

However, on the night she taught me to fight and consume marijuana, we were able to float away in a mist of amnesia and find peace and acceptance with one another. I was thirteen years old, Yasmin was sixteen, and we were both lost little girls trying to make it through life. We raised the lyrics by LL Cool J, which were resonating into the night.

Chapter 7:
One Person in My Corner

My first day at Del Norte High School had just passed. Mom had just relocated us to our own one-bedroom apartment following another round of David's nonsense when I was a sophomore.

To be completely honest, I'm not sure whose garbage she was upset about; perhaps it was her own, and she was projecting that anger onto him. In any case, she and David were two people trapped in a poisonous relationship that continually impacted my life.

I put my hair back into a half ponytail as I got ready for school, wrapping a blue bandana around the gathered hair on top. Yasmn wasn't with me to check how I looked, but I had seen other people dressed in this way before. I thought it was cool and was certain that I would blend in. I noticed that the other students either obtained a ride to and from school or traveled in groups, but I had no alternative. I was concerned the neighborhood wasn't safe to walk to school alone since you can just feel it in your bones.

My haven at Del Norte High School was Rachel and the females in her circle. They adopted me and gave me the nickname "lil güera," which they used to refer to me.

I immediately understood what was necessary to survive. They thought the physical education activities were pointless and a waste of time, so I frequently skipped class to be with them. We would relax and smoke cannabis behind the school. I soon started skipping other classes and fighting. I discovered that being a good student was uncool, so I gave up on my drive to learn. I had to blend in. In addition, nobody ever looked over my grades.

My body was starting to take shape at this point, and thanks to Rachel and my new pals, I understood that I could look both attractive and tough at the same time. That combination was ideal. Don't mess with me, cute. I adapted this look into my own with assistance from Rachel and a few of the girls whose makeup I had studied in class.

I used to spray Aqua Net or Rave hairspray all over, almost choking myself, then scrunch my waist-length mane into a curly mess with a towel after applying LA Looks Gel. I would use a diffuser to dry my hair. The bigger and crisper the hair, the better, was the aim. My mother detested the way I wore my hair. She told me her trick for using Sun-In to lighten my hair because she wanted me to look more natural. By this point, I had fully embraced the moniker "Blondie" and was pleased to be a distinct, blond Mexican. After all, I had red headed Mexican cousins. Why not go blonde? We come in a variety of hues and sizes.

I stopped wearing unisex skater clothing that was too big and started wearing more feminine clothing that showed off my form. I can now see that some of my earlier wardrobe decisions were a response to Mom's style. She wore tight clothing meant to catch the eye of men, which to me appeared to be flirting with danger. I was already being catcalled at and being observed when I was fourteen; why draw any more attention? I therefore chose the complete opposite. I didn't want that and would choose something else entirely if it appeared sexy. But now that the tide was turning, I felt at ease flaunting my physique. most of the time, at least.

One day, David saw me trying on Mom's previous stripper costumes to see how I was beginning to fill them out. He proposed taking some pictures while we were still residing with him. I pondered, "Why not?" But after that, he made me feel provocative. He requested me to bend over in one of her scanty dresses, and I felt uneasy. He motioned for me to lift my behind for the camera, "A little more," he added. David has always taken care of me and been my guardian. This photo shoot felt odd and unsuitable. It perplexed me. When Mom first saw the pictures, she was shocked by their sensual overtones. Nevertheless, David was my father, and despite how occasionally frightful or unsettling he may be, I also loved him. He was flashy and kind when he had money, and he was entertaining when he wanted to be. He astonished me in ways that made it possible for me to continue loving him despite everything else.

He was so bizarre that he gave me a gift in a large box on my fifteenth birthday. It had a saddle inside when I opened it. I couldn't understand as I stared at him. He knew that I had loved horses my entire life. When I was a child, he was the one who bought me doll horses and dollhouse furnishings; I would play with them endlessly. I was obsessed with all things equine and would have done anything to own a horse, but I never specifically requested one. Early on, I had discovered that asking for goods almost always resulted in rejection. However, for my sixteenth birthday, he gave me a horse!

The following weekend, we traveled together to pick her up and bring her home. She was a diminutive painter with a colt. I confined the two within a weak chain-link fence in the yard of an abandoned house across town at David's request. I addressed her as Sundance. She immediately turned into my entire universe because she was the closest thing I had to a buddy at the time. I took the bus to the abandoned house after school every day to take care of her, brushing, washing, and feeding her. Because I believed it to be too harsh to put a bit in her mouth or a saddle on her back, I would instead spread a blanket over her and ride her bareback with just a rope around her neck. I thought I was the luckiest girl alive as I rode through the neighborhood waving to the young children. Being responsible for Sundance kept me away from the gangs, drugs, and males that my friends were starting to get involved with.

However, the site where we kept her was awful; it wasn't a true stable, just a typical yard, and it wasn't exactly appropriate for boarding a mare and her colt. David always did things half-heartedly, and today was no different. Other people must have noticed the horses because it was just an abandoned house with a chain-link fence and no one there frequently to check on things. Sundance, however, changed after that. To keep her safe, we relocated her to a suitable stable next door, but she soon grew despondent and difficult to handle. She ultimately buckled and stood all the way up before smashing down on the ground to throw me, so I had to use the bit and saddle to ride her. She was devastated by the death of her child. Soon after, Sundance's condition plainly deteriorated as she grew listless and stopped eating. I presumed a broken heart when I heard that she had died. The loss of her altered me. Without Sundance to care for and adore, I became disoriented.

I counted on Rachel and her pals to protect me from bullying and brawls at school. I immediately realized that getting close to the tough girls provided protection. I was a sponge, learning how to appear intimidating and unbeatable. Even though I was terrible at it, I eventually discovered that if I was kind to the mean girls and shrunk down for them, they would protect me, just as David stopped hitting me when I pretended to be meek and silent.

I established a morning routine with Rachel. In order to keep Mom from finding out, I'd "borrow" her white Nissan Sentra and drive there to pick up Rachel. I'd be cautious to park the car in the same position and to leave the keys where Mom had hidden them the night before. We would then walk the six blocks to school together, watching out for one another.

Is it any surprise, then, that I took out my frustration on the first female who gave me a strange look in the corridor when I arrived at school? I swung at her with fingers that resembled claws, wanting desperately to be the victim of the violence for a change rather than the aggressor. I kicked, punched, hair-pulled, and scratched. My veins were dripping with venom. Never in my life had I been so irate. I'm not sure what I would have done if our peers hadn't forced us apart.

Later, during counseling, I picked up a saying that clarified this relationship for me: Hurt people hurt people. That is precisely what was taking place.

The principal of the school threatened to summon my mother and David to his office, but they had never visited any of the schools I had attended. At this time, they weren't planning to. When David revealed that he'd discovered a new rental house—a big one with numerous bedrooms!—and offered Mom and I to live with him again, a week of the school trying to attract their attention was resolved. I believe I simply changed schools rather than deal with the chaos at Del Norte, but it's also possible that I was expelled with a phone call. In any case, David's new home was close to Valley High, my third high school (the first was Sandia).

The funny thing was that, despite everything that had happened that day, Mom and David chose to act normally the following day. Everyone went on as if I hadn't been beaten to death by David and that my enraged reaction to that beating hadn't resulted in my expulsion from Del Norte. I used this as a means of survival. It was "avoid and bury," not "forgive and forget." Make my relationship with my parents okay and suppress anything that was difficult so that we may resume living our lives. What would happen to me if I let them both experience the full force of my rage? Without someone by my side, I might collapse totally.

Up until this point, I had only been concerned with surviving, getting by day to day, and trying to figure out how to defend myself and whether anyone had my back. Fortunately, that was about to alter. It was nothing short of transforming to have someone who loved me without conditions, who embraced me for who I was, and who wanted the best for me.

I can't recall how Angel and I originally connected, but I do recall seeing her at my new school, where I spent weeks observing her. By the time I started at Valley, I felt a little more secure in myself and at ease searching for the place I wanted to belong. Angel had an allure to her, an independence about her, and a self-control I admired. She was quiet and focused; she was so naturally though that she had nothing to prove. Without a care in the world, she strolled through Valley High's corridors.

Angel didn't seem to need to fit in with the jocks, stoners, cool chicks, or troublemakers; instead, she seemed to be a planet with her own orbit. I had become weary of hanging out with the tough girls at Del Norte and was no longer interested in always attempting to blend in and dispel the impression that I was weak. I didn't feel like myself, though. I have to continuously reduce myself to fit. I didn't want to be a part of a group at Valley High that needed me to be someone I wasn't. Angel had worked out how to achieve that, as you can see. I might also pick something up.

One day I smiled at Angel and she smiled back. She was surprised by how gregarious I was, and we hit it off right away. The junior year was this. We soon began sharing lunches and spending time together before and after school. Angel was athletic and came from a kickboxing family. I went to the dojo with her and studied under her. We laughed and competed against one another while exercising and perspiring till our hair dripped and our breath was labored. It felt wonderful. Although my physical strength and power increased, the inside changes were far more significant. I no longer felt like I was the victim of my circumstances. In the gym, I vented my resentment and rage, purging my body of all the conflicted, irrational feelings that had made life difficult.

She enjoyed having me around as well. We were able to discuss the difficulties we each carried and divert each other from the tension that came with home life while her mother was going through a divorce. Together, we experienced acceptance and tranquility. We talked for hours on end and never got bored of each other. Everything was made easier just by the knowledge that one other person knew me so well and was aware of my difficulties. I had no idea a friend could affect such a change.

In addition, I cherished my time spent there and frequently stayed the night. She had a real family, a strong group of individuals who watched out for and took care of one another, despite her mother's divorce. Together, they prepared and ate meals. Angel's mother was all I had imagined a mother to be. Before we went to night, she would sneak a peek into Angel's room to tell her to go fetch her favorite shampoo and conditioner; when we got up the next morning, we would find it in the shower. Every time her mother was there, I swooned. Angel had everything that I coveted.

I pretended not to hear what she had to say. I minimized it, just like David had been beaten. Whatever abomination Mom provided, it passed straight through. I also understood how dramatic Mom could be. Anything she did or said when she was furious couldn't be taken seriously. When she was upset, I would occasionally look at David, and he would give me a small eye roll and remark, "It's not as bad as she's making it seem." Every time I contrasted his composure with her hysteria, she appeared even more insane. Whatever you may think of David, he had the ability to maintain composure for the benefit of the young child present.

Mom and I shared a bedroom in the new home, which was down the hall from one another. On the other side of the house, David entertained a line of women in his room. I had become tired of it by this point. I had regularly experienced love at first sight with several of his prior women, especially Charmaine, Karlotta, and Wendy. I had gotten to know these women and their kids well. I refer to Alexandria, Karlotta's daughter, and her as sisters; we are still in touch. And Wendy, who was always nice to me, used to drive me to her night lesson in sign language. I became the ideal playmate for her daughter Tess. These women gave me what little motherly care I knew how to give. After the inevitable separation, they vanished, leaving me yearning for the maternal affection they had provided.

One day, we were in the new apartment with a woman David was seeing. She seemed to be becoming way too at ease with her position in the family and was discussing her future with David in the future tense.

In the meantime, I believed that I had stopped fighting at school. But one day, reports of a major altercation between Yvonne and Devina, two of Angel's cousins, spread across the entire student population. The story was that one of the ladies had dissed the other. Everyone believed that because Yvonne was older and had been out of school for a while, Devina would beat the crap out of her. She would fight to keep her reputation intact because she had to defend it.

Maybe Devina thought I'd be a simpler mark. She obviously wanted to stay away from the larger, older Yvonne, who Devina couldn't hope to defeat. I appeared to be an excellent stand-in target as I had essentially been adopted by Angel's family, including Yvonne. Despite my fear and conviction that she would beat the living crap out of me, I threw my hair up.

Thanks be to God for kickboxing. I immediately knew how to use the force Devina was exerting on me to counter it with a rapid left hook when she flew at me from her automobile. I just acted out of instinct and terror; I had no logical understanding of what I was doing, yet it was effective. Devina was confused, which gave me the opportunity to take her by the hair, toss her to the ground, sit on her, and begin whaling. However, Angel soon removed me. Watching her best friend abuse her relative couldn't have been simple.

After that altercation, Angel and I took on the role of the school's anti-bullies. Girls turned to us for protection against the actual bullies. When I put my hair up to fight that day, it wasn't what I had in mind, but after that, I was able to let the tough-girl act go. It turned out that I was tough; I no longer needed to act that way. Now I can have fun and enjoy myself. But I still felt horrible for Devina.

Angel and I were having too much fun hanging around, and nobody asked us about our studies, but I still had poor scores. By this point, Angel's mother had been so preoccupied with the dissolution of her marriage that she had stopped calling to see how we were doing in school. Naturally, my mother was not interested. I used to compose an explanation for why I wasn't going to school and get Mom to sign it. Because she was half sleepy, she didn't even bother to read the notes; she simply signed without asking.

On a balmy fall afternoon in the midst of the summer, Angel and I strolled home from school while the ground was warm beneath our sneakers.
Mom was typically just getting ready for the day when I got home from school, with sleep still in her eyes and her hair in a disarray. not now.

We slipped open the back door, and what we saw shocked us. They had created a mud bath out of the pond with the hose, splashing each other and screaming like kindergarteners given full reign with finger paints. Mom stood in her bikini top and thong when she spotted us, her expression the naive joy and naïve bliss of a seven-year-old.

The women below cheered Angel and me on as we ascended the tree that overhung the pond and cautiously made our way out on one of the branches. We held onto each other as we stood hesitantly and bounced up and down on the limb, taunting fate until the branch broke away and we plummeted into the pond. We were encouraged by their clapping. Although I still have a scar on my wrist from that incident, neither of us were seriously wounded. We laughed so loudly that we could hardly breathe, and that is what I remember the most. Mom also shows me love.

She visited me where I was after the fall and cooed over me. She had a tendency to be overly affectionate by nature, which she heightened when she was aware of her weaknesses in other areas. She tried to compensate for the fact that she wasn't the world's ideal mother by giving her children excessive amounts of attention. She usually made me a little numb with her gushy emotions, but today it felt fantastic. Mom and I were once again in agreement.

She continued on saying, "My baby, my precious baby," while giving me tight hugs and body kisses. I devoured it. After that, I would have been down to take a mud bath with her every day. Her unrestrained affection was a balm for my wounds.

Chapter 8:
Guys Are the Answer

Miguel Quintana was the most attractive man alive. Everyone was familiar with him because he was the school's standout quarterback and had graduated a few years prior. So well-liked, hip, and lovely. He seemed to like me, and I was really smitten. I found it hard to believe. Me. He favored me! We began spending time together at his residence with several other young people. We started making out all the time pretty quickly, but I stopped it before things got too serious.

I admitted, "I'm a virgin." I was fifteen years old and wasn't sure if I should be proud or ashamed of that. I mostly pondered how he would react to such information. I was more concerned about keeping him from feeling abandoned. He took a moment to think, and I almost heard a smirk twisting his lips. Well, I would love to take your virginity, if you'll let me," he said with a question mark in between. I didn't have any specific issues with having sex or keeping my virginity. Everybody around me was doing it, and I knew that having sex with him would make him my boyfriend and solidify our relationship. And I really liked him. Exactly why not? "Okay," I replied. Although there was no true romance and I wasn't in love with him, we had a decent chemistry. The truth is that I didn't really perceive him as a person at all because I had made up in my head a fantasy of who I wanted him to be and was so engrossed with the concept that he had picked me out of all the other girls accessible to him. I was unaware at the time, but this was the beginning of my urge to seek validation from boys and men through their attention and affection. My first use of drugs was Miguel Quintana.

He was kind and gentle the next time we were together. I recall bleeding and feeling extremely anxious after it happened. He even cleaned up the small mess we caused because he was being considerate. No one had ever explained anything to me, despite the hypersexuality of Mom's work and the life we had led. I was still concerned that if I masturbated, I would become pregnant at that point, and I temporarily had a fear of my own body. That's how ignorant and naive I was. Nobody ever taught me about STDs, contraception, or, more importantly, how to pick a reliable partner.

One day at lunch, Theresa, the cheerleader squad captain and one of the most attractive students on campus, came up to Angel and I. She was so stunning that it seemed as though a halo illuminated her from behind as she approached me. I was terrified since she was the most well-liked student in the school. Cheerleaders, in my opinion, were a different species than the wealthy bitches I went out with who could afford the necessary costumes and accoutrements. Because Angel and I were "real," whatever that meant, I had long assured myself that we were cooler than that crowd. To accept certain truths, you tell yourself whatever tale you need to.

"Stay the fuck away from him," I said, "that's my boyfriend." She walked away while turning on her heel and flicking her stunning hair. Strangely enough, I wasn't even angry—I was in wonder. Nothing made me happier than a gorgeous chick who could kick your ass. Later, Miguel claimed that she was a bitter ex-girlfriend, but I quickly realized the truth. No doubt, they were a couple. How could he refuse when I was simply a young woman offering him the chance to steal her virginity? He desired the prestige of being able to boast that a specific female would never forget his name (thus, I've altered his name here).

I shared the house with my mother, dad, and David at home, but that was about it. She spent most of the day sleeping and was out dancing every night. We avoided one other in the corridor and hardly ever spoke. I was a neat freak and constantly scrubbed the toilet and tub in the bathroom that we shared.

I sprang from my bed, gathered the sheets, and loaded the washer with them. I sent a note of apology to school because I felt so awful. "Will you sign this, Mom?" I entered her room on tiptoe, trying not to glance around since I was probably still smelling like puke and alcohol. I skipped class to hang out with Angel because I was still so sick and hung over after she signed it. Mom and David had no idea it had occurred.

On a balmy Saturday night, Angel and I were travelling in a convertible lowrider down Central Boulevard with one of her friends. We were exchanging Olde English 40 ounces and blunts while admiring the hydraulics and paint jobs of all the automobiles parked alongside the street. We were also looking at other cars and the people inside them. We spent our Saturday nights doing this, and for once we were fortunate to have a seat in her friend's car that had hydraulics. Cruising up and down the avenue while we bounced and the driver fiddled with the switches was the coolest feeling in the world. While everyone saw us go by, we maintained the calmest, most unflappable expressions on our faces. We were too cool to act happy or excited. Just remain calm.

An attractive older cholo was looking at me. He approached me and started talking, flirting, and paying close attention to me. Rudy was his name, and he was attractive but a touch on the small side. His automobile was equally stunning. He wore Dayton Wire wheels with a low profile. I found him to be strong and calm, kind of like David, I suppose. He gave me his full attention, as if I were the only lady in the parking lot. My cheeks started to warm up from the attention. It was pleasant after Miguel Quintana's disinterest. I gave him the scrap of paper with my pager number that I had scrawled on it out of my purse. He had a cute grin on his face.

That evening, when we were back in Angel's bedroom, we discussed Rudy and broke down the event. He was so focused, it confused me. When I questioned Angel about her opinion of him, she dodged the question. Rudy quickly established himself as my official boyfriend, the one who publicly embraced me and was prepared to fully assert his claim. I felt my value validated. He was incredibly attractive, and he exuded a quiet confidence that I found fascinating and enticing. He always had the perfect fade with a slight pompadour on top, and I adored the way he styled his hair. He took just as long as I did to blow-dry and hair-spray his hair. I was delighted to be his girl since I adored everything about him.

Rudy shared a small single-family home with his father, Thomás, and his younger brother. The front yard was made of dirt. Because everyone tracked dirt into the home, that yard was a nightmare.

Sandals would only make my feet dirtier from the sand. I yearned for the thought of a front yard with grass and a concrete driveway. I quickly grew to detest the dust in that location, but I ignored it because Rudy was my guy.

Rudy wasn't going to let me go to my senior prom. We proceeded to the off-site location where the official prom photos were being taken while dressed as if we were going to go in order to make me feel better. So that I wouldn't look taller than him, he made me wear flats. He was just maybe an inch or two taller than me, so there was no way I could wear heels with him. The closest I've ever come to a prom or homecoming was those pictures. But I didn't give a damn. I was in love with my guy. What more could one ask for?

Naturally, this new relationship gradually eliminated Angel from the picture. Rudy was very controlling and needed me available to him at all times, so he didn't want me hanging around with her. If he discovered that I had spent time with her, he would be furious and treat me badly.
The other factor was Angel's dislike of Rudy. Now, though, when we crossed paths in the hallway and she motioned for the charade to begin, I shook my head and refused to participate. She eventually gave up attempting to connect with me.

I had made a decision. My dearest friend would not matter; I would support the man. I was grieved to watch the happiness Angel and I previously enjoyed fade, but wasn't that how the world operated? Mom had never valued her boyfriends more than her friends or even more than me. In addition, I acquired a full family in the trade of Angel for Rudy.

Thomás, Rudy's dad, was a great father figure to me and was extremely wonderful to me. He had diabetes, was underweight and short. He regularly checked his blood sugar and gave himself shots. He and I occasionally spent the entire night curled together on the couch watching TV. If my dad had been more typical, I imagine that things would have been like this. He helped me feel loved.

We had no way to communicate with each other, so I was hesitant to notify Mom. These days, we hardly ever recognized one another's presence, yet this felt significant. Juana took a chance by alerting me. I should have at least made sure that her efforts weren't in vain. Additionally, I wanted to be somewhere else if a raid was about to take place. She and David might be able to deal with what was about to happen, but not me.

The next day, when I returned from school, the house was in utter disarray. There were moving boxes everywhere. I questioned my mother when I found her about the purpose of the packing crates. She announced our relocation to Boston with calm. I was aware that wouldn't occur. Mom wasn't a high school graduate. David hadn't either. I wouldn't either if I went with them. It's a marvel I'm still in school, but I was adamant about finishing. I somehow thought that unless I had a legitimate high school diploma, I wouldn't be able to find a serious job. I only knew that I wouldn't become like them.

I sprinted inside his home as soon as he pulled up, hiding behind the couch where Thomás was lounging. Rudy went after her and shut the entrance.
Her tires scraping against the curb made it sound like they were right next to my ear. She screamed, and I heard it on the porch. Give me my daughter, please! My daughter is missing. Minka, please leave the area immediately. Thomás had little knowledge of my personal life, but he rapidly assessed the problem. He advised me to keep quiet. She was now pounding on the door and yelling for me to leave at the top of her lungs.

I didn't even pretend to reject Thomás' offer once I had collected myself and realized what he was giving, as politeness might have demanded. I dialed David right away. Later that day, Thomás called David. "I'll require some sort of legal custody. I'll have to initial paperwork like permission forms for school. Mom met with Thomás in an Albuquerque law office; I'm not sure when or how, but she turned my custody over to a man she didn't know without asking questions. Two days later, she and David departed the city.

Chapter 9:
Not This Guy

I say, "Hey, baby." Rudy called out to me from behind the door to the bedroom we shared in an extraordinarily lovely voice. "Come on over here."

Just after getting home from school, I threw my bag on the dining room table. He had dropped his work boots and socks the previous evening, and they were now all over the living room carpet. He had the day off.

I've been housekeeping ever since I moved in with him and his family. Nobody asked me to; it was just a means for me to support myself. For my own mental health, I also needed to reside in a spotless home. I cooked for them, cleaned the fridge, and scrubbed the kitchen sink on a regular basis. I took the vacuum cleaner's hose attachment with the tiny bristles a month ago when I first saw the walls appeared dingy to see if I could make them look better. When a bright, spotless wall stripe suddenly emerged, I was startled. It was covered in dirt all everywhere! Cleaning only the walls took days, and then I had to deal with the awful bathroom that we all shared. How long had the three guys lived there without having considered cleaning the bathroom?

Rudy and our buddy Nina were seated on our bed when I opened the door. A half-empty bottle of Jack and a six-pack of cola left sticky circles on the dresser. Rudy seldom ever drank alcohol, especially during the day. On the bed, they were seated next to one another.

Nina didn't attend school with me; I believe she has graduated or perhaps she has quit. We were initially acquainted solely because she was the only friend Rudy let me have. But as time went on, I grew to love and believe in her. And it was now obvious that Rudy also liked her.

Typically, he was calling me a slut and criticizing my attire. He had grabbed one of my favorite skirts last week and thrown it out because he thought I looked too good in it. He tried all in his power to isolate me and make me completely reliant on him. He constantly cautioned me to avoid Angel because "she's a bitch." He gave me clear instructions: He, his brother, or his father were the only people I could travel with.

With embarrassment, I started to sweat. This man and maybe the other workers had seen my naked body in inappropriate poses; they might have also known the pictures were child porn because I was a minor. I returned home with nothing. After that, Rudy decided we should do live-action rather than using a video camera—voila, no need to have anything processed!—and made the decision. To be able to follow along as the tape was being recorded, he put up a tripod and monitor. He art directed the entire session while playing "The Boy Is Mine" from Brandy's most recent album, Never Say Never, in the background. He was quite invested in it.

I pulled up my top to reveal my breasts at the beginning of the film, assuming that was what he wanted, and I then addressed the camera. After that, it grew more raunchy, but what I remembered most was that I was acting and speaking like a young child when he demanded we watch it a few days later. I'd known for a while that I'd altered my conduct to appease him—what else could I do?—but watching it on camera made me cringe. Not me, that. I had gotten so good at leaving my body when things got difficult that I hardly even recalled recording the tape. The footage, though, stayed with me. Instead of a woman overwhelmed with passion, a young girl was acting in order to protect herself on the television.

We were able to avoid the rules that stated I had to be an adult to give my assent to such art since the tattoo artist was a friend of Rudy's. I absolutely left my body when it was time to expose myself for his needles because I was so terrified of what we were going to do. Additionally, I couldn't believe Rudy would allow another man to touch me while he was anywhere near me without wearing underwear.

While Nina and Rudy started kissing, I rubbed my cuticles. I simply sat on the bed and pretended to be somewhere else. They soon took off their clothing and started having sex next to me. They had completely forgotten about me, so I stayed right next to them, dressed. I had to leave since I was feeling unwell so I could rest on the couch. I grabbed my belongings and contacted Angel before the sun rose in the morning in the hopes that she would forgive me. She promptly grabbed me up along with my bag of clothes.

I asked her to stop at the drugstore on the way to her house so I could buy a pregnancy test. I had been experiencing nausea for a while. I feared that I was in trouble. When Angel and I took the test, the results were positive. Shit. I was unable to inform Rudy. He already had such power over me. This would solidify his authority over my body and me for all time. Instead, I gave my mother a call.

Mom finally arrived as promised for once. But I started crying when I was lying on the examination table. "This isn't what I want," I declared. The nurses were incredibly kind and hospitable. The doctor stopped once he realized what was going on. Before Mom spoke to us on the way home from the clinic, I was feeling better and wondering if there was any chance I could become a teen mother. "You know, we could carry out the plans my mother and I had made. both of us. We could take care of this child together.

I recounted Angel the entire tale when I returned to her home. As I called to schedule yet another appointment, she held my hand. Angel took me this time, and I followed through. I left with information about the importance of getting Pap smears every year, a bag full of condoms, and booklets outlining the various birth control methods I might use.

She looked after me when I got back to her place, and we reestablished our tight relationship. I wish I could claim that I stayed with her and realized what a mistake Rudy was. I wish I could say that I opted for this trustworthy girlfriend instead of that jerk of a boyfriend, but I didn't. I was confident that things would change as soon as I was capable of doing so and after enduring enough of his pleading for a second chance and for me to return home. I left Angel's home and went back to Rudy's. In a Stockholm syndrome-like sense, I missed him.

I then told Mom over the phone. Although she appeared joyful, she later said that the rest of David's family, including my aunt Sofa and David's sister, were not happy about the reunion. That dude is only a sperm donor, nothing more. We were responsible for raising Minka. They were justified in feeling that way. But I didn't give a damn.

I accepted a hair stylist's offer in the area as I was getting ready for Rick's arrival. He had volunteered to cut my hair for free and was David's friend. He was the most well-known hairdresser in the area and the one that everybody sought out. Although his kind offer made me feel a little uneasy, I wanted to look nice for Rick. My appointment was scheduled for after the salon closed. "It's just so you won't be charged," he said.

Indeed, he kept moving the gown aside to see my back while he cut the back of my hair, but as he reached the sides, he pushed the robe down in front, causing it to drop and expose me. He restrained my hand as I attempted to pull it back up. "You have no justification for hiding. Your breasts are lovely. Instantly, I went cold. I was terrified and by myself with him. Would he try to hurt me? I was unable to move. The other side of the garment was then pulled down, and he fondled me while complimenting my beauty. I remained still as I stood there, my body shaking with fright. It could deteriorate at any time. I still don't understand why he backtracked. He may have understood I was still a child, feared I might tell David, or simply noticed how terrified I was, but eventually he let me pull up the robe and cover myself. I appreciate the haircut, but I have to head home right away.

A few days later, I was out the door and in the front seat of Rick's red vintage Jag before he could unbuckle his own seatbelt. I turned to look at him. He put some Al Green on as we were driving through Albuquerque, which was my first exposure to the blues and soul music. He didn't play Whitesnake or Guns N' Roses, the rock and roll bands my mother liked. Tupac, the Fugees, and Too Short weren't the rappers I was listening to when it happened. I had never heard anything like what he was performing, and through the music, I instantly fell in love with him. I had never met a guy as cool as him. We went to get ice cream and then drove about while chatting—not about anything major, just us vibe-ing and getting to know one another. I was at ease around him. I hadn't experienced that in such a long time. He stayed for a few days and left me with an inheritance check from his mother. He sowed a seed before setting off on his journey back to Los Angeles. "Let me know when you're ready to leave this place," she said.

Rick gave me a check for $4,000, and I spent it on a turquoise Chevrolet Beretta. I felt very mature. I had some independence because of the might of that vehicle. Maybe I wouldn't be in this situation indefinitely. Maybe I had a second chance at life. After high school, I made plans to enroll in the nearby community college, but Rudy became enraged at the idea.

On an oppressively hot summer day, Rudy brought me with him to his lawyer's office. He was suing the county for a matter that concerned his line of work. While joking around, he and the lawyer somehow came up with the subject of males taking advantage of young ladies. I had been silent the entire time and had no intention of speaking, but all of a sudden, the story about the hairdresser came out of my mouth.

I hadn't known until then exactly what had transpired or that I was entitled to compensation. I might be able to have my own place even sooner if I win such a case. More importantly, this knowledge gave me confidence. These two men claimed that if I said, "What you did to me was not okay," a judge and a court would take my case into consideration. I had never been able to correct someone's treatment of me. I experienced motivation and elation. I intended to defend my own interests, finally.

Chapter 10:
Never Again

The heroine makes her decision and sets out on the journey, but escaping a painful past doesn't always happen in a large dramatic fashion like we see in movies. Sometimes there is a little back and forth, along with some wavering and hesitating and sporadic reversals. But as long as her overall trajectory is upward, we can be certain that she is moving in the correct way. That journey began for me when I eventually moved into my own apartment.

The rental was ordinary and was surrounded by other tightly packed apartments that I had passed on the way to work. It was the biggest apartment building around, and I reasoned that if they were that huge, maybe there would be space for me. I kept my word to myself and left the peep show after working there for six months because I was determined not to go down Mom's rabbit hole. The money was good, to be sure, but I had saved enough for first and last in shoeboxes stashed under the bed Rudy and I shared. To stay any longer was to run the risk of being seduced into that life permanently. Thomás, as he had promised, accompanied me to the leasing office for the apartment building.

Rudy didn't believe me when I informed him that evening that I was leaving. He had believed that I couldn't function on my own all along. He believed that my work at the peep show was a titillating side job I did for fun—something he enjoyed. He was unaware that I was saving for a move. He wouldn't have permitted me to keep my work if he had known. He preferred being in charge. In addition, he had provided me a way out. When I first mentioned to him that I was thinking about going to community college, he advised me to look for a new location to live. It was the ideal justification even though I had only graduated from high school a month earlier and had no idea how I was going to pay for it or even what I needed to do to get into college (no one had ever suggested I take the SAT). I intended to enroll at a community college.

I was eager to move into my new apartment, especially since I would have a washer and dryer of my very own. For laundry time, I've always kept a hoard of quarters on hand that I've fed into machines in Laundromats or communal laundry facilities. I could now wash my towels and bedding as frequently as I pleased, and if I wanted, I could have clean linens every day. I could choose exactly how I wanted my garments to smell.

For the first time in my life, I understood that I could provide for myself and that I wasn't a burden to anyone. I didn't get this apartment from anyone. The only one who assisted me in getting it was Thomás, who said a small white lie. I had constructed this on my own.

What time do I want to eat? I got to ask myself these questions now that I was going to live alone. What do I want to see on television? How late do I want to stay up? What time should I get up? These were inquiries whose resolution had always been dependent upon another party. I'd be able to choose what I loved now.

I was eager to create absolutely symmetrical lines in the carpet that nobody but me would be able to mess up after purchasing my very own vacuum cleaner. I was planning to make this a special space only for me. I had actually succeeded.

I quickly found a legitimate job working in customer service at VoiceStream, now known as T-Mobile. I invested in brand-new attire that was neither sexual nor professional—nice trousers, attractive shirts, no jeans, occasionally a blazer—the exact opposite of the stripper costume. I felt so good about myself. I had my own desk and cubicle at VoiceStream, amidst a sea of cubicles, but it was mine, and I furnished it with a cork board that I had tacked with images of my friends, my mother, and myself, as well as perhaps a few motivational sayings. All the school materials I had always adored, including pens, pencils, pencil sharpeners, and highlighters, were all around me. I had a positive, healthy, and career-focused feeling.

The workplace was a gorgeous, brand-new structure with all modern amenities; it wasn't dusty and in disrepair like so much of my life had been. I had lunch with the other girls in the break room where we talked about our work and personal life. I occasionally enjoy this new reality by dipping my slice of pizza in ranch dressing when we went out for pizza at Dion's for lunch.

This existence was very different from anything I had ever experienced. I avoided talking about my previous job, sex tapes and sexual assault cases, how I learned how to keep a man slipping money into my slot at the peep show and how bad that place smelled, or the fights I got into in high school and how difficult it was to get blood out of my clothes afterward when I was interacting with my coworkers. It appeared as though none of that had ever occurred. All that mattered was the present.

I kept a close eye on the vehicles driving past the curb at LAX in search of Rick's recognizable car. I preferred his red Jag the most. The interior of it seemed tidy and sophisticated thanks to the brown leather. He had replaced the Jaguar engine with a Chevy engine that produced serious horsepower, and the steering wheel was made of solid wood. He treated the car like his own child, giving it the care and upkeep it required. In an instant, I could choose it from a lineup of Jaguars. When he pulled up, I was standing there with my two large luggage and my hand to my forehead to block the light from my eyes. I agreed to travel to Los Angeles for a week at his recommendation.

We struggled to fit all of my bags in the trunk, but as soon as I sat down, we resumed our conversation and music-listening session, thoroughly unwinding in each other's company. I immediately relaxed when we got to the West Hollywood home where he and his wife, Robin, lived. Robin was an artist who worked for Jim Henson's Creature Shop, and Rick was a musician. Their creativity was evident in every facet of their daily lives. The house was serene, with plants all everywhere, music playing, and unique and eccentric furniture. The aroma of patchouli and incense was a constant in the home. Rick had a guitar stand next to the couch and would play quietly while watching TV or conversing; he was nearly always holding a guitar. He and Robin also appeared to truly love one another. She tolerated his stupid, goofy, lively, and humorous behavior in such a way that I could see she loved him. They had a chemistry that I wasn't used to noticing: mutual respect.

Rick and Robin took me to Catalina Island on that trip, where we rode bikes around the island despite becoming a little seasick on the ferry. Then Robin showed me where she sold her little paintings—some on canvas and some on ceramic tiles—at the Fairfax Flea Market. I used to roam the market looking for hidden gems while she was working at her tiny booth.

I had figured out by this point that I was a fish out of water. The girls in Los Angeles appeared effortless and gorgeous, which is very different from how we conducted ourselves in Albuquerque. Rick used to become frustrated with how long it took me to get ready whenever we had plans to go anywhere because I was wearing a lot of makeup at the time. I dressed up and left my room one morning. His face was marred by shock. We're only going to Home Depot, Mink.

Rick's startled and humiliated expression as the waiter left made me feel bad. This was his special place, where he was addressed by his first name and where staff members always brought him his preferred latte without him having to ask. And here I was, dressed in attire that was utterly unrelated to the West Hollowood mood, with long, airbrushed acrylic nails, a well contoured face, and a thick Albuquerque accent. My favorite movie at the time was Mi Vida Loca, which is set in Echo Park, which is pronounced "Echo Par-qué" in the film. That's where I might have blended in, but in West Hollywood, I felt like an alien.

He still enjoys telling the tale now. I believe it was when he began to respect me. Unfortunately, it was also a time when I was reminded of a lesson I had already learned: I had to be a certain way in order to get love. Simply put, I wasn't enough as I was. I had to be liked by men; I had to make sure no male ever felt ashamed of me.

When my trip to Los Angeles came to an end, I bid Rick and Robin farewell and headed back to my job and comfortable apartment, but there was something strange when I entered my living room. The enormous entertainment cabinet and the black velvet couch lost their cool factor. In a way that was unfamiliar to me, my existence appeared constrained and perhaps a touch run-down or dismal.

Chapter 11:
Busted

While the officer ran my ID, I looked in the rearview mirror to check my cosmetics. I could not believe that I had been stopped for speeding. That fine would be painful to pay. In order to pass the time, I removed the mascara from underneath my eyes. I felt anxious. I've always been afraid of the police.

On a Friday night, my buddy Tricia and I were driving home after going out dancing with several coworkers. I had on a one-piece denim jumpsuit modeled after Frankie B, heels, sizable earrings, and a ton of makeup for a night out. I didn't drink and I looked good. I knew we'd be leaving as soon as the officer gave me the ticket. However, the officer appeared more serious when he returned to my window than when he had initially pulled me over. Step outside the vehicle, he ordered.

I was instructed to take my clothes off at juvie, take a shower, and wash my hair with Dial bar soap as a female guard observed. Then I was required to put on their uniform, which consisted of large scrubs and gigantic, baggy, worn-out underpants. Nothing matched. My jewelry, handbag, and all of my clothes were taken away. It was late at night when I was finally led to my cell. I climbed onto the small mattress on a concrete bench and the guard pointed at me while a girl slept in one of the beds.

I spent the weekend in juvenile hall since I couldn't see a judge until Monday morning. Tricia was unable to save me as a result. I later discovered that the other females had committed relatively minor offenses like shoplifting once or twice, fighting with a parent, and running away from home. They cried out when they learned I was facing many assault charges. Wow, you're screwed.

I heard the other girls' experiences throughout the course of that weekend, some of which shattered my heart. For instance, my buddy cherished his time in juvie. She made a point to visit there as frequently as she could because she didn't want to return home. She considered this to be her home and these people to be her pals. She could only rely on Juvie to provide her with a healthy supper three times every day and to make her feel protected. I knew I had a difficult upbringing, but at that moment I realized it could have been worse. I recalled the phone number of the attorney who had been involved in the hairdresser case during the booking procedure. He was sympathetic when I called him on the one phone I had, and he promised to meet me in court on Monday. Now, the only option was to wait.

I was given two years of community service by the judge, who then released me. Despite having had tougher charges made against me, I felt bad because, compared to all the girls I had met that weekend, I was going off almost completely unscathed. The majority of the girls I left behind would receive the book as a punishment. Help was really what they needed. They required attention and nurturing. They required new habitations. to be a student. Nevertheless, the deck was loaded against them.

I had already lived in my apartment for a year when my lease expired a few months later. I had the option of committing for an additional year or changing. By that time, I had realized that Albuquerque didn't offer me much beyond unpleasant memories. I hadn't seen David in a while; Mom was constantly traveling and staying at friends' homes rather than a set residence. Rudy was no longer in view, and Angel had found a man she was planning to marry. And me? The employment was still nice, but I couldn't afford community college while also making rent. I thought about my choices. This would be my existence if I remained in Albuquerque; it would go on forever and ever, amen.

I had assistance from Rick and Luciano, who was at the time my best buddy. As I said goodbye to everything that had become my life, I was sobbing uncontrollably, but I knew it was the right thing to do. Goodbye, Albuquerque! There wasn't much left there for me. She was once more stuck with nowhere to go. She was living there, sleeping on the floor of my empty apartment, in my mind. We had never lived in a nicer apartment than the one I had gotten for myself when I was eighteen. I affirmed to her. I threw myself inside the U-

Haul cab after locking the door one final time. My weeping ceased as soon as Rick moved the truck away from the curb. Relief and deep breaths were all that were left at this point. I was prepared to proceed.

Chapter 12:
City of Angels

I was looking for a spot to get breakfast while Rick and I were traveling along Fairfax. Soon after I arrived in Los Angeles, it was a late Saturday morning, and the sun warmed my face through the windshield. In anticipation of the day I would have my own apartment, I had kept my furnishings in storage since moving to Los Angeles in a place little larger than the one I formerly shared with my mother. I felt a certain amount of tenderness when I thought of that small place. Is it true that I ever called a storage container home? A garage, too? How much I had forgotten or purposefully repressed is incredible. I was eager to start a new and more fulfilling life for myself in Los Angeles.

I was captivated by the brightness that was seeping into the car as Rick drove into Beverly. This place has a special radiance that sets it apart from other places. Los Angeles has a somewhat different sun than other places; the atmosphere there had a golden hue that attracted me. I gazed out the window, soaking in my new surroundings and inhaling the aroma of eucalyptus and gasoline. But something about this day was different. Although Los Angeles is seen as a driving city, that wasn't necessarily the case. In Los Angeles, many people stroll. Just not as many as I was seeing at the moment.

She went to great lengths to make me feel at home in the house I shared with Rick and Robin. My living conditions were serene. When Robin would inquire, "Darling, have you put the kettle on?" in the afternoons, her British accent always made me smile. That cozy small aspect has remained with me ever since. The first and most crucial item in whatever room I occupy is my kettle.

Robin set up a bedroom for me, complete with sheets that were much finer than anything I had ever touched. I usually bought the cheapest sheets since I didn't realize how much a difference proper bedding might make in how comfortable I was. When I went out late, she placed a tiny small lamp on my bedside table and would turn it on so that there would be light when I got home. Such minute nuances were very important.

I tried to learn from Robin while she wasn't looking, but I kept it a secret. Issey Miyake perfume and minimal makeup were used by Robin. She had a fascinating job designing "creatures" for the film business and was an artistic, self-assured woman. She later worked on a team that designed many of the creatures seen in the film Where the Wild Things Are as well as pretty much every other furry creature you've ever seen in a movie. We painted together in their living room back then when we had free time in the afternoon. Compared to her artwork, mine was like a stick figure drawing. She could draw the most incredible patterns on anything I pointed to in the room and asked her to paint it for me. On so many levels, Robin captured my heart, and she taught me how to be a woman in this world without having to submit to a man. She was entertaining and had a sneaky sense of humor. Given how elegant Robin was and how much she enjoyed beer, any notion that she may be stuffy or dull was dispelled. Robin was able to hold her own in her relationship with Rick. I enjoyed that she was the family's primary provider.

Looking back, I can see that I hadn't taken into account the fact that living expenses in Los Angeles were more than 50% greater than those in Albuquerque. I was prepared to start working though and felt fairly certain that I would figure it out. I had planned to visit the AT&T call center at Hollywood and Vine as soon as I got there on Monday. I had my resume and references prepared and had printed out the directions from MapQuest. VoiceStream was a small, local business; AT&T would undoubtedly be an improvement with, I hoped, higher salary.

However, the offices weren't anything like the opulent ones at VoiceStream when I arrived. The entire department was located on the unattractive basement level of a run-down building in Hollywood. I initially questioned whether I got the address correctly, but after checking again, I came to a different decision. Maybe it wasn't as exciting to work for a cell phone company here as it was in Albuquerque.

Naturally, I accepted the position. I had a job to do. I would now, however, also need to look for a second job. The AIDS Healthcare Foundation required me to spend my afternoons performing community service as atonement for the judicial system from when I was arrested, so I didn't have a lot of spare time. I was concerned that I would never be able to pay off the debt because it took an absurd amount of time over the period of two years.

Every morning at five I made my way to the dismal AT&T offices, but instead of taking calls from customers and being the magical godmother who erased their debt, I was told to make incoming solicitation calls. I was bad at it and despised every minute of it. I was aware that at this rate I would never be able to purchase my own home. I had agreed to a deal with Rick and Robin for a month, but now I see how unreasonable that assumption was. In Los Angeles, very few teenagers can establish themselves within a month.

I went to the Beverly Center to fill out applications for a second job on a day that was difficult on many fronts. Since I began working for AT&T, I hadn't closed a single sale, and I was afraid I would be let go. I felt absolutely out of place as I spent hours at the AIDS Healthcare Foundation filling papers after that morning shift. I was starving by the time it was evening and hadn't eaten in hours. I would have accepted any job that paid well.

After I completed the application at the Guess store, the assistant manager invited me into a back room for an interview. Green eyes and caramel skin made Marie look stunning. She seemed in charge and yet very nice despite being a few years older than I was. I made an effort to respond to the question directly, but somehow the entire chaotic tale of my life and this dreadful day spilled out. My resolve had worn thin. I unintentionally spilled my guts to Marie because I was hungry and exhausted.

I was employed there and then by Marie. My experiences with Marie changed everything about living in Los Angeles, and that job quickly emerged as a high point in my life. She quickly established herself as my closest friend, guiding me through Hollywood life and correcting me when I made a mistake. Even now, whenever I'm about to take a risky action, I can still hear her voice saying, "Minka! That is not something you can do! That is unacceptable. Her corrections never felt violent or like a parent reprimanding me since she would laugh at the ridiculousness of whatever I was saying or doing while yelling at me.

She was the first person who ever cared enough about me to call me out on my bs. When I was slow on the pickup, she didn't give up on me and had the grace to realize that, if given the chance and room to progress, I would. She removed my rough edges by telling me what was right and wrong about the way I interacted with others. I had essentially spent my entire life battling for survival. I was quite impulsive, and it didn't take much to rile me up. I learned from Marie to take a deep breath, to understand that not everyone was out to get me, and to react from a position of calm and centering. She essentially taught me how to behave as an adult who was not raised by wolves. She saw me and loved me without ever passing judgment. I could feel it.

I was frequently ill by this time with colds, bronchitis, and whatever else was going around. I was doing phone solicitation from 5 a.m. to 1 p.m. every day, followed by my community service job from 2 to 5 p.m., before going to the store to work from 6pm until closing and working there until 1 a.m., resetting the displays, cleaning the store, and making sure everything was perfect for the crew the following day. With all these demands on my time, I wasn't sleeping enough, couldn't eat well or frequently, and was a little agitated.

I re-started my life, this time on my own, by moving into the apartment that was next to hers. Rick was still making me mad. But it turns out Rick was correct. He received my thanks afterwards. He got me to go on by setting the law, and I needed that. One of the best times of my life was made possible by living close to Marie; we had a lot of fun together while she taught me so much about cooking, dancing, boys, and movies. Rick had also taught me a more tough-love attitude when he asked me to move, even though his manner was less empathetic. Marie always treated me with gentleness.

Mom continued to reside in Albuquerque, but she frequently traveled to California to visit her friend Kim, who resided in San Diego. After visiting Kim, the two of them would go up to visit me in Hollywood. Kim was a close friend of Mom's from the world of strippers, but their lives had developed in different directions. Mom was now a cashier at a gas station, and Kim was wealthy because her husband had started a business that produced dolls—at first simply torsos—that were modeled after her and the other dancers she worked with. His business prospered over time and eventually began producing life-size dolls. These would develop into RealDolls, or lifelike sex dolls, and thanks to their success, Kim's standard of living significantly increased. She nevertheless made time for Mom and treated her like a sibling.

I informed Marie about Kim's proposal a few days later. Marie, who had dabbled in modeling, knew of a photographer who offered free sessions to actors and models in exchange for their time, and she advised me to have some headshots taken. I could choose whether or not to accept Kim's invitation after I met them, and it wouldn't cost me anything. I have a photo shoot coming up soon. Even though I was still unsure if this was the best course, I would at least give it a try.

As requested, I brought my own clothes to the photo shoot, however Tina, the photographer's wife, took care of my hair and makeup instead of me. My hair was fashioned in a softer, more natural way, and she reduced the intensity of my heavy makeup. Tina talked to me while she worked on me. A lot. She told me that she had once been a Playboy Playmate and that she now oversaw the careers of other models in that industry. She offered to speak on my behalf.

She nearly spit out her coffee when I informed her that I was working a ludicrous amount of hours per week, including community service.

She persuaded me to quit my work at Guess because Marie had just accepted another position and it looked like a good time to do so. I would now take calls in the plastic surgeon's offices because of Tina. Tina ran the surgeon's office as well as guiding the careers of aspiring models. You can take calls when I set them up for you because the hours are flexible, she said.

I'll tell you what. I'd been working there for about a month when Tina arrived at my desk with a calendar. "You are scheduled," I said.

Tina has been advising me, preparing me to join her portfolio of models, and recommending various plastic surgery procedures to increase my chances ever since I started the job. She stated that because I worked for the doctor, he would perform the treatments for free. I required a lot of treatment, said Tina, but we'd start with liposuction, breast augmentation, and veneers for my teeth.

She held up a calendar, and I just stared at it. Both the liposuction and the breast augmentation, which were scheduled for just a few weeks apart, had my name listed. I wanted to disagree. I wasn't sure I wanted to go through all that, and I didn't really want my body to be messed with, having witnessed procedures firsthand. But Tina had treated me so well. Perhaps she had the finest judgment.

Marie and I would frequently prepare dinner together and talk about our days. She adored it when I cooked for her because she was always so impressed by my ability to transform Top Ramen into a more upscale dish (thanks, Mom). We made pho, but it wasn't the mouthwatering version we enjoy now because we were in our 20s and living in studio apartments, and we had a blast doing it.

"Minka, your boobs are exquisite in every way! Those boobs would make people kill. Your current state is ideal. Your boobs are not being fixed! I apologize. I'm not going to take part in destroying your body. No way." I informed Tina that I needed to postpone the operations the following day at work after hearing Marie's advice. The only person who always had my best interests in mind was Marie. I believed she was correct and trusted her.

But the following day, when my shift was over, I was asked to come into the surgeon's office. Tina was also present and was in front of him. He appeared to be studying cue cards that she had penned for him. I was in awe. I turned to face Tina. She didn't express sympathy with a straight face, indicating that this was her fault. I was sorry to lose this employment, but I wasn't going to allow myself to be pressured into changing every aspect of my physical appearance. I was unaware of it at the time, but this experience that I perceived as a rejection turned out to be yet another chance for development.

Chapter 13:
Boundaries Are a Bitch

For me, taking a stand against Tina was a wonderful accomplishment. Yes, I received my punishment quite soon, but I remained unfazed. Making that leap signaled that I was coming into my own in some way.

I devoted a significant portion of my life to being what other people wanted me to be, always willing to bend or twist to fit their needs. But things were beginning to shift at this point. I started to get my first, very first ideas about the kind of life I wanted to create for myself. I was certain of the following: I desired independence from others and the ability to sustain myself. I desired a serene environment in my house as well as a meaningful job. I had absolutely no aspirations of becoming famous or an actress. I set out to live a straightforward but deeply satisfying life, and I made progress in that direction. But it was challenging. Getting your priorities straight with yourself can have a negative impact on your other relationships. Others may not always be pleased when you set boundaries.

While the letter was being delivered to Kim, I fretted and waited, hoping she would share my perspective. I held my breath when she called because I was terrified she may say no or that she might have changed her mind. Nobody has ever made such an unconditional offer to assist me before. I wasn't certain if I could believe it. Mink, oh Mink. Even though she wasn't as animated as usual, her voice was quiet. I regret hearing that you don't want to be a model. You have a lot of potential for success in that line of work, and I don't believe you completely recognize or value your own beauty. However, I will undoubtedly support your goal of becoming a nurse. Go ahead, honey. I have your back. For the first time in weeks, my shoulders were able to relax as my heart beat faster with excitement. I knew how to proceed.

I started going to school and absolutely adored it. I spent six hours at a time, on the weekends, studying in the Beverly Hills Public

Library. I simply cannot express how wonderful it felt. Like the other students, I took around anatomy and physiology textbooks in a backpack and worked incredibly hard, recognizing for the first time that I was intelligent. This was a second chance in many ways, allowing me to make up for my time in high school, when I frequently skipped classes in favor of merely getting by. After elementary school, when being interested in the world around me was no longer cool, I pushed away my need to study, but now I was able to indulge it. Kim and the fact that my rent was paid allowed me to give all of my attention to my brain so it could process what I had just learned. I surprised myself with how well I could recall material and understand challenging topics. I grew once I allowed myself to experience that urge to study once more.

I was paying a visit to Rick and Robin. After mending fences, we now made time for one another whenever we could. I was pacing the living room when Rick pressed the button on his answering machine. The sound I heard, the sentence from his machine filling the air, confused me. The voice seemed both weird and reassuring. That inflection hadn't been used since I left Albuquerque a year prior. The dialect from that area is really distinctive, and as it came out of his recorder, it sounded like I was hearing it for the first time. Had I been found at Rick's by one of my old friends?

I consider that period to be a crucial component of my ongoing journey to understand who I am as an adult and how I came to be this way. It astounds me that even now, as I work on this book, I continue to find evidence of the indelible marks left by this period on my mind. Now that I'm deeply planted in Mexican culture and this family that reared me, I can see the positive aspects of this time period. I truly appreciate and celebrate the emphasis on the family, my upbringing in terms of etiquette, loyalty, and respect for authority figures, as well as the food. Albuquerque is the only location where you can find Hatch chiles, and there is no flavor quite like those there. The most frequently asked question, even at McDonald's, is "red or green chili?" There is no one type of race or ethnicity. This is just to convey something that helped shape who I am now, not to essentialize Mexican culture.

I took anatomy and physiology for six months before spending the following six months getting real-world OR experience. I spent a sufficient amount of time in the school's fake operating room before being transferred to California Hospital, a low-income hospital in the center of downtown Los Angeles that is situated between the Staples Center and Santee Alley, where imitation designer products and clothing are marketed. Until my teachers determined I could do procedures on my own, I followed another scrub nurse.

I was initially given a job in the central sterilization and processing department, where all surgical instruments were cleaned, prepared for sterilization, and then put back into their containers after being scrubbed clean of blood and tissue. They were all very disgusted when I described my day to anyone. But me? I couldn't wait to enter the operating room with a task in hand and see how the tissue got there, where the blood came from, and how the blood got there.

I progressed from cleaning tools to eventually working as an attending in the operating room, where my responsibility was to foresee the surgeon's demands and immediately meet those needs. I discovered that the doctors preferred to talk to us about their spouse's meal the previous evening or their round of golf rather than the current surgery. They would know I wasn't doing my job if they needed to discuss the surgery at all. I was resolved to complete this task as skillfully as I could.

People don't fully understand how difficult and intrusive C-sections are for the lady undergoing them. During my time in the OR, I learned that it's a trauma that is unappreciated, and it left me in awe of the female human body's miraculous ability to withstand such stress.

I was there on this specific day to help. A surgical drape prevented the patient from seeing what we were doing even though she was conscious and her husband was present in the room. The doctor used a knife to initially pry open the skin on her bloated, taut tummy while we blotted, suctioned, and cauterized to stop any bleeding. I made sure there was no blood in the area and gave him the tools he required when he needed them. He carefully cut the layer of subcutaneous tissues that was next to be exposed. Finally, we reached the uterus after passing the oblique muscles (I won't go into detail about how we pass those muscles here in case anyone reading this would need a C-section in the future).

I had been following along up until this moment, seeing what the surgeon was doing, wiping away blood so he could see, and acting like a silent, consummate professional. When he cut open the uterus, everything was different. The amniotic sac, the final barrier separating us from the fetus, was there, cradled in this woman's pelvis, completely intact (her water hadn't burst), and inside it, a fully formed, exquisitely matured, adorable child was visible to my eyes. An individual! I felt privileged to be there at this transitional time between being a developing human being and birthing a complete, prepared-to-join-the-world person.

There was no time for awe in this kind of procedure, so the scrub nurse startled me out of that state of wonderment. A C-section is a minimally invasive procedure that moves quickly. The delivery accelerated when the amniotic sac was severed. We needed to have the baby out as soon as possible at that point; the doctor wasn't talking about going out to dinner with the spouse or playing golf. A pediatric nurse was given this completely developed, stunning human being with flowing black hair so that we could attend to the mother and treat the wound. Her entire uterus was removed by the doctor, who then placed it on her chest and stomach. Before the doctor put the uterus back inside the patient, we utilized gauze and damp sponges to clean up every inch of it. We then sew up the following layers we'd cut to facilitate the birth. This wasn't a simple procedure, and whenever I overhear someone minimize the difficulties a woman faces during a C-section, I make sure to point out every detail. I go into great detail on how we bypass the abdominal muscles and reach the uterus. Typically, this lesson puts individuals (typically guys) back in their proper perspective.

During my tenure at California Hospital, I saw every type of procedure imaginable besides open heart surgery, and I discovered that surgery is essentially carpentry. I cherished every second of it. I once held one end of the saw as the surgeon and I dutifully cut the section of a homeless man's foot that would have eventually killed him if left intact during an amputation procedure. I was really grateful. This was the definition of doing an honorable job.

I completed my education and received the top honors, after which I began working at an outpatient orthopedics facility. The compensation wasn't spectacular, but I loved the variety of surgeries we performed at California Hospital. I'd have it easier at the outpatient center if I was committed to being self-supporting and had a schedule that didn't require me to be on call 24/7, so I went there.

Chapter 14:
Old Patterns, New Resolve

He was so appealing that I found it difficult to look away when he initially entered the suite at the Staples Center where I had been invited to watch a basketball game with friends. Sean was his name, and I fell in love with him right away. I made an effort to hide it, but I believe he was aware. But in our first meeting, he was a bit of a jerk, and that put me in a good position. I would treat him like any other person—a buddy of my friends—and proceed from there.

I started going out with Sean and my buddies on a regular basis. He and I eventually began to regard one other as more than just friends as a result of our increased one-on-one time. I do believe that the fact that we were just friends at first was a great blessing.

Together, we had a ton of fun being silly and ready to turn anything into a game. We required food, right? We would make a visit to Ralph's, the silliest conceivable outing. washing clothes? Let's have a blast at the laundromat while quoting Jay-Z songs! We both had an abundance of joy in our hearts and were quite youthful, usually acting silly and exuberant and enjoying each other's company. We were in our twenties, carefree, savoring every second, and spending as much time as possible with friends.

I was a nurse at the time, working full-time, and I was content with every aspect of my life. It was a terrific friendship with Sean. I was prepared when he asked me to move into the home we had chosen together. I let go of my apartment and carried the same furniture into the house we shared that I had taken with me from Albuquerque. We were creating a life together.

I was anxious when I got to Jackie's office, but I kept telling myself I didn't give a damn if she loved me and wanted to sign me. Just so Mom and Kim would quit bugging me, I took this action. After looking at me closely, Jackie and her employees briefly discussed something.

Kati took me into a room where she taught me how to "find my angles" as she took Polaroids and demonstrated how to posture. Before I knew it, she was sending me to castings for work where it was acceptable for me to be five foot five and where models were needed from the shoulders up, including beauty ads, accessories at Macy's, and a few music videos.

Even while the work wasn't particularly exciting, it was a wonderful addition to my nursing salary, and Kati is still one of my closest friends. Soon after, Kati introduced me to a commercial agent, and I began attending commercial auditions. Because I worked early in the day at the orthopedics center, I was able to fit this work in around my nursing duties. The music videos and modeling were just side jobs to supplement my income. I didn't take anything seriously.

Sean and I watched news reports about people relocating displaced Louisianans into their houses after Hurricane Katrina that year. These were folks they had never met before, but they needed aid. Even though we couldn't do anything in the moment, there was a sense that we all needed to look out for one another.

In the meantime, my mother had been expressing her desire to be close to me and how much she missed me. We frequently wrote letters to one another, and although we could have stayed in touch by phone and online, there was something special about getting one of her letters, with her handwriting on the envelope seeming so familiar and wonderful. The way she formed her letters almost made me feel her mood. She desired to travel to L.A. at this time to be nearby.

Our home, where Mom, Marie, and I all shared a roof with Sean, was like a TV program about quirky roommates getting up to crazy antics together. Mom took a job as a courier and drove throughout the town, dropping off scripts and delivering items here and there. She returned home each night to tell us about the bizarre things she had seen. We all got together every evening after work and had a blast. Everyone adored my mother because she was so devoted to them, calling everyone "my baby" and "my love," and expressing her affection for Sean and Marie. They also adored her. It was easy to love her. When she was healthy, she was nothing but unrestrained enthusiasm, joy, and love. It was lovely having her in the house and we had fun together.

On our days off, Marie and I (and occasionally Mom) would wake up early to climb Santa Monica's steps before eating cinnamon-sugar pancakes for breakfast at The Griddle Cafe on Sunset close to Fairfax. We were regulars, so the employees gave us tips on off-menu treats like the Supercalifragilistic, which was French toast topped with frosting and covered in sugar and cinnamon. We chatted, perhaps did a little window shopping, drove about listening to Jay-Z's Reasonable Doubt or Kanye's The College Dropout, or we went to a movie at the ArcLight on Sunset. On other days, we went to Zuma or Venice beaches to relax. Alternatively, after dining at El Compadre, we danced until two, three, or four in the morning. Mom was like a huge kid with Marie and I, joining in whenever she could.

Mom prepared the majority of the food for our feast that Christmas, including our beloved stove top stuffing and other dishes made entirely from boxes. Along with mashed potatoes and turkey, she also prepared yams with marshmallows and brown sugar. She even completed the entire decorations, including the living room Christmas tree and stockings for each of us. Even though she was never very adept at cooking or managing her life on a daily basis, she adored holidays and went above and beyond to make them special. She would have preferred that we not have invited Rick around for Christmas, but when she found out that he and Robin were divorcing, she made an exception.

Rick had sat me down a week earlier to tell me the entire tale. He said that Robin had been having an affair. I was enraged at her. How could she? They had the only relationship that appeared to be in good shape that I had ever seen, and now she had destroyed everything. I was furious.

Mom's old habits returned after they had been cohabitating for a while. She insisted on saving money for an apartment, but she didn't seem to be going to work as frequently as she once had. She was staying in her room more often, munching on those medications like gummy bears.

Her OxyContin use was getting worse, but I was unable to convince her to change her ways when I tried to talk to her about it.

Mom had been napping or watching TV in bed all day long for days on end when we were a few weeks into our second month of living together. She was frequently still wearing her pajamas when I got home from a hard day at work. She didn't appear to be making plans to depart, so when Sean brought it up, it prompted me to take immediate action. I developed a strong sense of duty to defend him and our bond. I needed to talk to her in a really trying way.

I could now see how Rick had been able to tell me the same thing. Everybody must eventually be able to stand alone. Even though I wasn't yet aware of it, he had noticed that I was prepared. And now Mom would need to prepare herself as well, in some way. She wasn't a teenager, either. I was working on building my own life and was sick of being the parent in this situation.

But boy, was she irate! She snatched her handbag, threw on some clothing, and stormed downstairs, smashing doors as she went. I soon heard her car squeal as it left. I had the horrible feeling that she still had plenty of anger in her.
She called a little while afterwards. "Come on over. Sean, me, and you for dinner this evening, okay? like the old days. We'll discuss everything.

We had an agenda. Before Mom got home and we all went to the restaurant together, I told Sean the specifics. He and I agreed on the best course of action to take in this situation. Mom didn't seem overly upset that evening, which surprised me, and I began to believe that we would be able to resolve this conflict without causing too many wounds. But inside the restaurant, where the aroma of the exquisite bulgogi beef I adored filled the air, she started eating before we had a chance to place our orders.

She didn't arrive at her house until after one in the morning. Had she had some sort of transportation or had she walked that far to get home? I overheard her collecting her belongings in her bedroom and then fumbling to get them all into her car. She rejected my help when

I walked outside to offer it while wiping the sleep from my eyes. I won't ever forget that evening. She was standing next to her car while the roadway was being slowly invaded by fog and deep shadows were cast by the vaporous mercury lights. Then it was over. I was through. I had established my boundary and was prepared to stick to it. Because she was my mother, I had to put up with a lot from her, but I couldn't take it anymore. Now, in order to be honest to myself, I was ready and eager to accept her rage and her abandonment.

I was completely committed, and even though I did all in my power to distance myself from her, I would be lying if I said I didn't sob myself to sleep that night.

Chapter 15:
Acting Class

Uncertain of my purpose, I sat in the acting/theatre course in the dark. I was encouraged to enroll in the class by a friend because I was now frequently acting in commercials and music videos. Exactly why not? After my shift at the surgery center, I was able to attend the afternoon lesson. I was only beginning to understand the course.

The rest of us sat in the darkened room and watched, noticing subtleties in the players' conduct while our teacher, Janet Alhanti, offered acting exercises to pairs of actors who entered the stage on this particular day. She demonstrated the Meisner approach, and we engaged in a "repetition exercise" where two actors sat across from one another and one actor said, "You're smiling." The scene partner then concurs with the first and reiterates what was stated. I'm grinning. The practice gradually gets more complicated when mood and conduct are added.

The exercise's goal was to urge each actor to concentrate on the other rather than on themselves, and to refocus their attention from the words they were using to the emotion that was driving the conversation. It was intriguing to observe how the performers' stiffness decreased as the exercise progressed and how intense emotions started to surface. The performer just had the present-day vulnerability to work with, soaking up every nuance and emotional input from their scene partner. The actors occasionally grinned or laughed; other times, the tension increased. Although the exercise may seem simple, it can actually be rather challenging. The tiny alterations in vocal intonation, meaning, and interpretation of uttered words, along with variations in mood and the atmosphere in the room, occasionally caused the actors to become upset or cry. Sometimes all it takes to make someone cry is prolonged eye contact and being seen without being able to hide or divert.

Everything about it attracted me. That is, until my name was called and I suddenly found myself on stage, with all eyes on me and a young man seated across from me, our knees touching and our eyes locked. I was unable to move because I was so afraid. My body was probably trembling. I wanted to get away because I felt naked and raw. I wasn't prepared for this level of intimacy with a complete stranger, much less in front of other strangers.

I used to be able to hold back my emotions so I wouldn't give someone else what they wanted, but now they just flowed unhindered down my cheeks. I shrugged as I covered my eyes from the lights since I didn't want to respond to that question in front of the entire class. However, the main reason was that, up until this point, I had never really even given the possibility that I had been mistreated as a child any thought.

I was happy even though I was crying. even ecstatic. Maybe for the first time ever, I had been noticed. Janet was able to cut through all of my barriers and find the true self that was lurking inside. Her care and concern for me made me feel good and nurtured. Who I was and what I might develop into. I had felt completely exposed and stripped bare in the heat of her attention. But I also sensed that perhaps I could now fully unwind. I might simply be myself. No matter who it was. In that instant, all I knew was that I would stick with this woman and learn everything she had to offer me.

When I did so for the first time with another person, it was difficult and draining, but I persisted, and soon I felt myself beginning to change. The acting classes completely captured my attention, and I made the decision to devote my entire life to learning the craft.

Additionally, I felt like I had finally found my place in the world for the first time. It was finally safe for me to express all of these emotions and to experience the anguish that I had long rejected and repressed. I began removing all the layers and discovering who I was. Even while I don't think acting should be used as therapy, I now see how learning about myself and how to stop hiding behind the masks I had developed to survive was undoubtedly the beginning of self-awareness, even though I wasn't conscious of it at the time. In either case, I was addicted.

It was a good kind of being swallowed up. In those days, I believed that if anything didn't hurt, it wasn't worth it, even if exploring my psyche in acting classes hurt like hell. the areas that were sensitive? I had to go down much further there. There was more to learn about there. I did, too.

I developed a fierce loyalty to Janet, who I followed around, attended every class she offered, allowed myself to be open to the process, took private lessons from, and taught me how to be open and honest about my feelings and experiences. I took a seat as close to Janet as I could as she normally sat in a dim area against the wall. I wished I could hear every word she said. I wished I knew everything about her. I was eager to find the woman she claimed was inside of me. She often said things like, "Sensitive people change the world, and the rest don't give a damn." I wanted her to like me, of course.

I discovered that I had created a survival strategy that I employed anytime I felt threatened. I became a small child with a tiny voice. That was done to make sure I wouldn't get wounded and maybe even get some help. That was how I had gotten by so far in life. They may not hurt you if you're small and seem innocent or defenseless. This was done totally unaware. I'm embarrassed to admit that I still have trouble sleeping because of the voice. To speak from my diaphragm when I'm scared or intimidated, I have to remind myself that I'm safe and relax my throat.

I soon received a job as a guest star on Amanda Bynes' television series What I Like About You. I worked on a few episodes and was terrified, insecure, and scared while on site. I genuinely shook when I said my lines. I would record the shows and then watch them alone when they were broadcast because I didn't want anyone to see. I would then reflect, "Hmm, I need to loosen up."

I appeared in commercials for Clean & Clear and Old Navy, both of which also starred Kristin Chenoweth, which completely frightened me. I had recently seen her perform in Wicked on Broadway and knew every word to every song. She was known as Glenda the Good Witch, and in my opinion, she was a divinity. I was totally awestruck.

Fortunately for me, the character I was portraying in the advertisement had to speak quite quickly, so I got the ideal opportunity to let all of my anxiety out. It all came together flawlessly, and I still adore that advertisement. Despite the fact that none of these positions were very outstanding, I was still moving forward.

About a month later, my agency contacted me with another possibility. A TV series based on the feature film Friday Night Lights was planned. Did I see the movie?

Of course I was aware of the movie! At least six times, Sean made me watch it with him. He was intrigued with the football players in that small Texas town and the challenges they had to overcome because it was one of his favorite movies. He was a sucker for underdog stories and enjoyed those individuals in general. I, on the other hand, had no interest in football whatsoever and had no real desire to be a cheerleader. I took a chance since, if everything worked out, Sean would be in for a pleasant surprise. Not only would I be able to help pay the bills, but I would also appear in a show based on his favorite movie.

From him, I kept the audition a secret. He wouldn't be disappointed if I didn't get the part. And suppose I did succeed? I'd open a bottle of champagne, tell him everything, and give him all the credit for helping me get this far. He would be overjoyed.

I was pleasantly delighted when my agent contacted me to tell me they wanted to see me again after the first audition. Really? Although I wasn't convinced it was possible, I wanted to allow myself to think I could obtain the part. I didn't get my expectations up because I was still so new to this world and because of all the no's I was now used to.

But after a few weeks, I began to believe it because the numerous callbacks went above and beyond what I had anticipated, giving me the chance to try to impress the producers and, eventually, Peter Berg, the writer and director—the man, the myth, the legend. Nevertheless, I worried that every callback would be my last since they would replace me with a stronger actor after noticing my undeveloped acting abilities. But they continued to phone me.
Everything had changed by the time Pete and I were in the same room. The callbacks had all been doing the same scenes in the same way up to this point. Pete, however, was not interested in that.

He didn't care that we weren't experienced actors; he was more interested in our ability to perform. to follow instructions and improvise, as well as to make quick notes. He looked confident that I could do it, and I had a blast. The following step involved a "chemistry test" with Scott Porter, who was competing to play Jason Street, the standout quarterback for the Dillon Panthers. They were interested in seeing how well we got along on camera. Scott was a great guy who made improvising a breeze. I sensed our affinity right away. That particular day, I felt pretty good as I left the room.

But things weren't so fantastic at home. Sean seems very reclusive. I had no idea how to close the gap because this had been going on for a while. When someone has made the conscious choice to distance themselves from you, how do you invite them to be closer to you? By this time, we had been dating for two years, and I thought we would be even closer. But something seemed odd. He left me nice messages and cards and told me how much he loved me, so I could tell he was trying his best to get us back to a decent place, but the distance kept widening.

I awoke early on a Sunday and crept downstairs to feed the dogs without arousing Sean. He owned a dog himself, and for my 25th birthday, he gave me Chewy, my cockapoo that I loved more than anything else. I scooped out their meal and saw his bright BlackBerry on the counter. I looked to see if he had a caller; perhaps it was an SMS from work that he wanted to respond to. If I'm being completely honest, I have to say that I needed to see that message, according to my gut. I don't like to spy on others, so this would be the first time I did it, but given how far apart we have been lately, I felt compelled to check.

I'm headed over to Marie's. I'll arrange for movers to pick up my belongings. The majority of the furniture, including the black velvet couch, was stuff I had transported from Albuquerque years earlier. I wouldn't give up on it. Even though Marie's apartment was just about 500 square feet and I wouldn't be able to stay there for very long, I realized I had to put my own emotional health first. It had taken me a long time to develop self-care habits, assert my rights, and come to the realization that I deserved respect. And I understood that only if I pushed for it would it happen. I left Sean's house and sobbed to Marie for days.

I had to be there to give them instructions as the movers arrived to take my belongings from Sean's house and load them into the U-Haul I had reserved. When I got there, he was waiting for me in the living room, contrary to what I had hoped would happen. He rushed out to hug me when he saw me, and as soon as he was in my arms, he began to sob. As he wailed, the movers moved end and coffee tables all around us. I'm not sure what altered it, but I felt powerful. I reflected on all the times my mother had rushed back to David when she truly wanted to be left alone and on all the occasions when I had rationalized poor behavior in my own relationships by assuming that's simply how things are. This stuff was meant to be tolerated by women. But that's over. I was through. My message to the universe was that I deserved better. And for once, I was convinced.

I sat on the couch in the living room and looked out the window at my full-to-the-brim U-Haul parked at the curb. I no longer had the inner fortitude I had at Sean's, and I could now clearly see the severity of my situation. I didn't know where I would reside, how long I would need to keep the U-Haul, or whether I should rent a storage facility for the furnishings. How was I going to make a living? If necessary, I could return to nursing full-time, but the idea of giving up acting crushed my heart. I was aware of one thing, though. I was very clear about what I deserved in life over the past few months. I bid my mother and her nonsense farewell. I was no longer willing to tolerate Sean's deception at this point. I attempted to convince myself that it was growth. This was advantageous. Was it not?

Chapter 16:
Friday Night Lights

I made for bad company since I was picky about my meal and unable to have a conversation. To try and cheer me up, my buddy Rose took me to Hamburger Hamlet on Sunset, but it didn't work. We were supposed to get manicures or do something similar to make ourselves feel better after, but I just didn't have the heart. I should have been more appreciative of her kindness, but I was such a mess. How was I going to make this all right? My chest felt so badly that I thought I could nearly feel my heart's internal organ oozing out into my thorax. I felt bare in every way.

I was sheltering from the gorgeous day in her car on the way home behind a large pair of sunglasses when my phone called. I nearly let the call go to voicemail, but I realized I had things to do, so I wiped my face on my sleeve and picked up the phone. Saying, "Minka, this is Mark." It was my boss. "I have some news for you." I was prepared for him to inform me that the arrangement for which I had repeatedly been summoned back had fallen through. Obviously, it had! I was having no luck.

I hung up and we had a little party in the car. I knew where I was going! There was a path to success! I had no lofty expectations for the program itself. It was merely a stepping stone in my eyes. Has a film ever been effectively adapted into a television series, after all? I didn't believe that. In addition, the series was focused on football. I didn't give a damn about football. It didn't matter what came next as long as I was prepared and knew what it was. The pain in my heart persisted, but I had the impression that I was recovering from a severe flu.

Rose drove me back to Marie's small apartment, where we danced in the living room while weeping and screaming after I told her the news. I repeatedly muttered, "Thank you, thank you." I thanked Marie for being such a terrific friend and for providing me with a safe haven during this trying time. I gave thanks to the universe for providing me with a break at just the right time. I expressed my gratitude to my agency, my acting professors, and everyone else who had assisted me thus far.

I even called the surgery center to express my gratitude to the medical professionals I had interacted with for helping me along the way. They had always made sure that I put in the necessary hours to get by while still leaving in time for my auditions. I assured them that I would always be a scrub nurse and that as soon as I returned from Austin, I would immediately join them in wearing scrubs.

I contacted a few friends to share the news with them, including a close friend named Cat who made me think of my mother. She was the least judgmental person I knew, a little older, free-spirited, and utterly open-minded. I adored her because of this. She also embraced everyone with complete passion, much like my mother did. I felt safe and cared for by her defending energy. Cat wasn't my mum, who I hadn't spoken to in a while, therefore she wasn't a replacement. Cat acted more like a supportive older sibling. She squealed and joined in my celebration as I gave her my news.

I packed my whole wardrobe into the SUV, leaving just enough room in the back seat for Chewy to stretch down on a blanket. My furniture would be shipped to Austin by the production company, so

I wouldn't have to bother about that. On a warm day, I picked Cat up first thing in the morning, and we both started driving. Cat and I alternated driving while enjoying music from CDs we burned and dancing inside the vehicle. We listened to Memoirs of a Geisha like a book on tape when we grew sick of music, even though there was no "tape" involved; instead, there were an apparently endless number of CDs.

We took pictures of each other, stopped in tiny villages to explore, ate all the junk food one would expect to find on a road trip, and laughed nonstop the entire time. Whenever one of us was in the passenger seat, she would always have Chewy cuddled on her lap and her bare feet up on the console, tapping out a rhythm to the music. When we had to relieve ourselves and there were no bathrooms nearby, we urinated by the side of the road— commonplace road trip behavior.

We arrived at the Texas border after an uninterrupted ten hours of traveling. I couldn't imagine we would go the same distance tomorrow while remaining in the same state. I never realized how big Texas really is. The company of Cat made all the difference the following day when the scenery was miles and miles of brown. By this point, I had moved past the Sean fiasco and was eager to start this new chapter. I was at peace with the fact that I didn't live with my mother. I was eager even though I had no idea what was going to happen.

When we first arrived in Austin, I fell in love with that tiny city. I had no idea what to anticipate. I had a mental picture of Texas as being arid and bleak from what I had previously seen and heard about it. Austin, though, was not like that. There are lakes and trees all around the city, and there is abundant natural beauty everywhere you turn. I had no idea there would be so much water!

The sights were all taken in as Cat and I drove around. Everywhere we turned, joggers and cyclists were zooming by. Everyone was very fit and healthy. Additionally, a large number of individuals were out strolling their dogs or dining outside with their dogs. Keep Austin Weird signs might be seen everywhere. My kind of place, it was.

I quickly saw that Austin was a place that prioritized music. Austin was teeming with musicians, which had such a different mood and nothing but advantages compared to L.A.'s abundance of actors, which had both benefits and drawbacks. Of course, it's simple for me to say that because music wasn't my line of work. I was able to naively savor everything the city has to offer. I saw that all the musicians appeared to play music purely out of passion, with no thought of fame or wealth in mind. They sang of the freedom in their decisions and the joy they felt in making the world more beautiful while performing every day of the week in practically every tiny dive bar for tips.

I received a few thousand bucks from the production firm to help me move. You receive a one-time relocation fee from production when you sign on for a regular role in a new TV program that shoots in a location other than your home to assist you relocate out and settle in the new place. You are then regarded as a "local" hire and are in charge of finding your own lodging and commuting to and from work. On the other hand, if you are working on location for a shoot, they provide lodging and transportation each day. Being a local hire, like I was, saves the production firm a ton of money and worry. The relocation fee is somewhat absurd because it rarely even covers the first and last months of rent for a new apartment in a new neighborhood, let alone a new city or, perhaps, a foreign nation. However, I was a young man, and it seemed incredible that they had given me any money at all.

Additionally, they sent me a list of suggestions for the new city, including wonderful housing possibilities that were close to any amenities I would require. With their assistance, Cat and I were able to locate an apartment for me directly on Congress, Austin's main thoroughfare. That was enough for me: it was tidy, had a kitchen, a bathroom, and a bedroom, and appeared secure. Right across the street was Jo's Coffee, a fantastic place for people-watching that serves the best coffee in the area and welcomes dogs by providing a jar of dog goodies at the pickup window.

Cat and I took a look at the restaurant scene and immediately understood we had struck gold. We became quite interested in the local Tex-Mex cuisine, particularly Austin queso, often referred to as chile con queso, which is said to be the dish that enables Austinites to thrive. It is a delicious concoction of melted cheeses and chopped peppers that occasionally includes extras like chorizo, guacamole, or beans. It is served with a generous portion of tortilla chips. I could eat that stuff all day long, and Cat and I pretty much did.

Cat and I went to Target after renting the apartment. We required blow-up mattresses, sheets, and kitchen supplies but the moving company wouldn't deliver my goods for at least a week.

After years of barely getting by, I was finally able to let my guard down a little regarding the price of the things I bought. I wasn't paid a lot by Hollywood standards under my new deal for Friday Night Lights because I was still relatively new to the industry and no one knew how well the show would perform. However, I was still under contract and earning more money than I ever had as a scrub nurse. I determined that I could afford to have fun on this particular day.

Cat and I browsed all of Target's houseware aisles together, adding items without checking prices or considering whether I might have found a better deal elsewhere. It was very different from the times I had gone shopping with my mom when I was a child, always fearful that we would have to return stuff if we went over budget. I didn't have to check my bank account twice today to make sure I could pay for the dishes I wanted. They went onto the trolley if I wanted them. Even though I don't think I spent more than $300 that day, I made an incredible haul. I got the impression that I was finally escaping the long-lasting financial instability.

Cat stayed for a couple of weeks while I adjusted in and left me on my own when she took out for L.A. I initially spent my days walking around the city, trying to eat at as many different restaurants as I could, and getting familiar with the area. I was the first cast member to arrive in town because I immediately went out after learning that I had been recruited. But soon more people started to arrive slowly, building up their own homes and lives.

Zach Gilford, who plays Matt Saracen in the show, was the first person I met. He and I hit it off right away and became good friends. We are still doing it today. He was cordial and really sweet, just like the character he played on the show. I adored the fact that he made a side income leading school groups on adventures in Iceland. He was just so awesome, in my opinion. For those first few days, it was just the two of us, so we would frequently get together to hang out and eat.

Adrianne Palicki, who plays Tyra Collette, was the following cast member to arrive, and I was thrilled to see her. "Yes, yet another girl!" I was excited to meet new people. She was entertaining, and we quickly grew close. She was a five-foot-11, stunning bombshell from Ohio with the sweetest smile and the happiest disposition— truly a girl's girl. She was also not quite as inexperienced in the acting industry as I was. I expressed how much fun it would be to get our hair and cosmetics done every day at one of our first dinners together.

I felt very at home as soon as Jason Street's actor, Scott Porter, arrived. He seemed like a friend to me right away because I knew him from the chemistry test. We would all go out to bars together as a growing group, drinking, hanging out, and getting to know one another. Everyone got along, and everything was simple. Soon, Kyle Chandler (Coach Eric Taylor) and Connie Britton (Tami Taylor) showed up. Jesse Plemons (Landry Clarke), Taylor Kitsch (Tim Riggins), and Gaius Charles (Smash Williams) eventually joined the cast. Although Aimee Teegarden (Julie Taylor) had also arrived in Austin, she wasn't really old enough to go out with us at night. I felt privileged to be a member of this crew as everyone there was thrilled to be there.

I was so nervous before we even started filming the pilot that I could not stand it. Even though I just had a brief line to say during one of the opening scenes in the diner, every time we got to that point, I would tremble with fear as I said my line. The strain was great. Okay, lady. Yes, this is now your show. You are capable of doing it.

I was completely out of my depth, but slowly I relaxed. I think it was a plus that Peter Berg, the filmmaker, could tell that I had the ability to play, could improvise, and could take direction well. However, I lacked any formal training and had very little set-specific experience. I was learning as we went and lacked confidence.

Sean had just betrayed me, and now here was this guy who was so attractive to look at and had a peculiar Canadian accent. There was strong chemistry between us. I fell in love with him right away. He wasn't too serious, was amusing, and had a lot of adventures. It was as though he was unaware of his attractiveness. His humility and groundedness dispelled any preconceived notions you could have about someone so attractive. He never failed to make me or anyone else laugh.

On-set and off-set flirting and laughter with him turned out to be the best medicine for my freshly shattered heart. We quickly and deeply fell in love. Back then, I would have told you that we were deeply in love. Yes, mad. However, it wasn't love. We had a crush on one another. Then, I didn't know how to offer or receive love.

Peter Berg once requested that Taylor and I join him for brunch. Taylor and I had shared the same bed that morning, but we had arrived at the restaurant at different times so as to avoid being seen together. Later, Pete claimed to be fully aware of the situation. He also understood that we would ignore his advice, but he had to try.

Since my mother stormed out of the house stating I was never her daughter during this period, I hadn't spoken to her. I attempted to ignore her requests for contact when she called and wrote to me, but I didn't pay attention to her communications. I wanted to make room for myself so that I could come to know who I was apart from her. All of her letters to me expressed her love for me, her missed me, and her regret for her actions. All of that might have been true, but I was sick of putting up with her. It was time to put myself first.

I can still hear her telling me those things. Baby, I have cancer. Everything happened all at once in a split second when I heard that. My body exited the room as my mind whirled around on its axis, maybe hitting the floor, and I searched for another body that hadn't just heard the news. Then, at that instant, every scenario and possible result flashed before me, and all of my body's survival mechanisms kicked back into action. I had to downplay this devastating information. Deny. Angry as well. Blame her for everything while I'm at it.

Of course you do! was my initial reaction. It is all about you. It's possible that she had a milder form of the illness, and she was planning to take full advantage of it by making me her victim once more and seeking me for aid. I was not going to be duped.

I was upset with her. And obviously shocked. Every time I started to stand up, she would appear, prepared to ruin everything for me. I tried my hardest to feel sympathy for her but failed. She had neglected me and was now neglecting herself, and I hated her so much for it.

Nevertheless, I enquired as to how the diagnosis had been made. She admitted to taking ex-lax and having been constipated for a very long time. She went to the doctor, but I'm not sure if she had insurance at that point. The doctor only gave her more laxatives. This continued for a while until the harshest laxatives ceased to be effective, at which point she saw a different physician. In her intestines, the more recent doctor discovered a tumor the size of a grapefruit.

His tone grew solemn. "The time is running out for you to resolve this. You need to resolve your grudge with her before she passes away because you two went through a lot together. In every other case, you will live to regret it. My world started to whirl. Despite my frustration with my mother, I still needed her. My desire for her remained unabated. I was unable to accept the veracity of what Rick and she were stating. My mother wouldn't pass away. That was impractical.

Chapter 17:
Cancer

In the first few episodes of Friday Night Lights, Lyla Garrity, who I played, sobbed a lot. She was doing everything in her power to aid her partner, who had recently been paralyzed. It got way too simple for me to cry. After the initial excitement of being a part of the show, I was pretty depressed due to my mom's disease, which I generally kept quiet about on set, and the cast member conflicts that were now beginning to develop.

I'm generally the one to break up relationships. Hooking up with me at this time was a lose-lose because my superpower is to flee at the first sight of either stability or turmoil. It was only a matter of time, regardless of the guy, until I dug up something to pick apart, something to make me think I shouldn't be with him. That is a problem I have. not theirs. Either I lacked the self-worth to realize I deserve the love in front of me or I lacked the self-worth to understand I'd be fine if I ended a toxic or emotionally unavailable relationship. Even though I was in continual pain and confusion, I kept falling back into that dynamic because it felt secure to me. That requires its own chapter in therapy.

Anyway, after breaking up with Taylor, I would pretend to be professional by grinning at work, while everyone else felt bad for the guy whose heart had just been shattered. Instead of taking me out for drinks after work to console my hurt feelings, my castmates took him out. To be fair, I didn't let anyone know how devastated I was. Taylor was far more adept at showing emotion and being open about it. He was incredibly aware of his emotions, whereas all I knew to do was put on a brave face and keep my stuff to myself. But as the results of both of our coping techniques show, vulnerability breeds connection. My tough-guy demeanor simply made me feel alone. Nobody will actually be there if you act as though you don't need anyone and that nobody around you knows any better.

I was quite lonely because I didn't know anyone in town other than my castmates, so I would rekindle our relationship to stop feeling so alone. Of course, that wasn't the only factor in our reconciliation, but it would be a lie to deny that loneliness had a role. I was delighted in our company. Simply said, the good only persisted for so long before our incompatibility manifested itself. We ended up breaking up and getting back together more times than I can count.

There is a limit to how many times you can avoid looking at or acknowledging someone on set before the director bellows, "Action." It was virtually hard for us to avoid becoming devoured by the chemistry we shared at that point in our lives. Sexual chemistry can be highly perplexing in your twenties. You're certain that you two are meant to be together if you have this kind of connection.

When my mom's illness was combined with the anguish of her condition—which, to be completely honest, I still didn't fully grasp or understand, though I knew it was bad—I had everything I needed to cause Lyla to cry on camera. All I had to do was put on my headphones, play "Fix You" by Coldplay just before they shouted "Action," and think of my sick mother and the stresses at work, and I started crying repeatedly right then and then.

The manner I was working on Friday Night Lights was causing my work to be disorganized and occasionally even a little overly dramatic. But as I already mentioned, I was studying on the job. No amount of acting classes will ever truly teach you how to work or what suits you unless you are actually on set. I wish now that I had listened to Peter Berg at that breakfast meeting.

In order for her to see what we were filming, I placed her up in "video village," the area behind all the monitors, and provided her with headphones. I would walk over to where she was sitting after every scene, and she would simply grin at me, silently clapping with excitement no matter how well or poorly the take had gone. I could feel the love coming from all across the room, even across an entire football field. Despite all of our past disagreements, I always knew my mother loved me and was extremely proud of me. She did a lot of modeling when she was younger and aspired to act; she had been in a few small roles. She was overjoyed to see me in the setting she had imagined for herself. Of course, everyone on set adored her and enjoyed her company.

It felt as though my former best friend had come back during this time. Because of the cancer, she had become more humble and yearned to be my mother in a brand-new way. Our relationship underwent significant healing during that period, despite the fact that she was ill. I was still very much in denial about how bad she actually was, though.

I carried her around the entire city, refusing to acknowledge that she was ill. I wanted to treat her, so we went shopping. When I was younger, my friends and I always enjoyed shopping at Target or Payless for new clothes or shoes. I wanted to do something nice for her now that I had some money. I just couldn't believe the fact that she was so weak in front of me.

I visited my mother in San Diego during a break in production. No one, no matter how large or small, loved animals or found more joy in them than she did, so I bought us tickets for a safari ride at the Wild Animal Park. We would be driven around in a van, so she wouldn't have to do any walking, and she would get to view her favorite animals. It was the ideal excursion. My strategy was a total success.

On our safari, she became as giddy as a child, and seeing the joy on her face thrilled my heart. She got to feed one of the giraffes when they got close, and her joy was contagious. She was letting these lovely creatures take leaves from her palm. I was so pleased to see her pure joy.

This time was such a relief from all the suffering Mom and I had experienced in the past. I was able to let go of all the grudges I had been harboring because of my disease. For the first time, I allowed myself to fully embrace the tenderness she had long shown me but that I had occasionally learned to rebuff. No matter what I did, I always felt her love enveloping me.

I see now that my perception of what love was was terribly distorted. All I had was her example. She struggled with addiction and was a dreamer, so she would do anything to get her fix—children and loved ones be damned—including steal, cheat, and lie. Not personally, just trying to survive. I thought that was how things were, at least.

I was perplexed at the moment because this clinic was my first experience of therapy. My mum loves me, of course! She loved me, therefore she kept me alive. I believed that she loved me as a result of all the crap I had to endure. To her, I represented the sun, moon, and stars as well as the oxygen she inhaled. She couldn't withstand ever spending any time apart from me. It was there, and I knew it was real.
I told the therapist that she was mistaken, but she insisted otherwise. "That is not the affection of a mother. A mother never puts her child's needs ahead of those of a man, drugs, partying, or anything else. Not that, it is love. I was at a loss for words. I resisted giving in. If I adopted this viewpoint, my entire universe would be upended.

She requested that I write down the dialogue I would need to deliver to her. I was apprehensive to do what the therapist advised because Mom and I had finally made up and were spending quality time together. Even yet, I wanted to handle things properly, and I believed that this therapist was experienced. She believed that talking to my mother would help me release something inside of me and would give me the chance to express all the ways I had been wronged. I recalled that this woman was a professional. I have to have faith in her.

I went up to Mom on my subsequent trip to San Diego when she was in bed, as she was frequently by that point. With her health failing her, she sat up to face me. She appeared to be a construction made solely of toothpicks, fragile and unable to support herself. And every last bit of dignity she still had was destroyed by my remarks, which were like sledgehammers. She already carried a great deal of guilt.

She was already aware of all the precise wrongdoings and errors she had committed against me. And there I was, in bold red letters, naming every single one of them for her.

Before my eyes, everything inside of her, much of which was already broken, crumbled to pieces. With each of my words, she began to shut in on herself like a building that had collapsed. She was ruined.

When I watched her shatter like that, I awoke from my reverie and realized just how miserable this poor woman was. She made an effort. She was a woman who had learned to rely solely on her attractiveness as a means of exchange as a result of the social conventions she had been raised with. She had no positive role models growing up. There is none. She had never experienced luck. As a single mother with no discernible talents, she had a difficult task to complete, but she made the best of the situation. She lacked a family to rely on and a place to retreat to. They all left her for her independent lifestyle and referred to it as "tough love." She loved me more than anything, albeit perhaps in a very imperfect way, but she loved me with all of her being.

Years later, I can now more clearly perceive the truth. She ceased acting as though everything in her life was fine once she was diagnosed with cancer and began accepting responsibility for her decisions. Together, we discovered the space for healing after that change.

Before my therapist offered her advice, we had already made significant progress toward a complete reconciliation. Despite her good intentions, my therapist's advice proved destructive. That day with my mother is among my most agonizing recollections, and I never went back to see that therapist again.

Mom and I were doing so well at the time for the first time in a very long time. I pleaded with the cosmos to extend our time together. To realign felt wonderful. I was able to get along with her so well. Give me some more time, please.

Chapter 18:
How Is This Happening?

At the beginning of that summer, Mom stated, "I can't do this anymore. It was 2008. She had grown weary of the side effects of the chemotherapy on her body and the way the medicines made her feel. "The doctor claims that if I continue receiving chemo, I will survive another year. I'll pass away in six months though if I stop. I'm not convinced this is worthwhile.

I listened to her as she weighed the advantages and disadvantages of this choice. I agreed with her decision to prioritize life's quality over quantity. It's all mine now. She was constantly miserable. On one of my most recent visits, I had spent the entire time waiting outside of the restroom as she puked. For her, it was painful and draining. She didn't have a robust enough immune system to withstand the damage the chemotherapy was doing.

She continued to suffer from the cancer every day even after ceasing the chemotherapy. This was extremely frustrating since I had my mother back in my life in a new way. She was curious about what I was doing, interested in my aspirations, completely behind me, and centered on me. My entire life, I had craved that kind of parental care, and suddenly it appeared like she was thinking exclusively about me.

I began to appreciate her as a woman and fellow human for the first time, rather than just my mother. She was a poor baby who had never received a break, and my heart ached for her. She had experienced only hardships, taking blow after blow after blow from life. She had made many poor decisions, to be sure, but she had also been dealt a lot of extremely horrible luck. My mom's return made me incredibly joyful. I could once more see her humble spirit since she was clear-headed, sincere, and pure.

Mom made the decision that fall to relocate back to Albuquerque. Kim in San Diego was wonderful and extremely loving, but she had four kids, and her home was constantly busy. Mom simply lacked the energy for such mayhem at this point, and since she spent so much time in bed, she frequently felt lonely. The idea of moving in with her best friend Holly was accepted because many of the people she truly loved were still in Albuquerque. Mom traveled back to Albuquerque without too much difficulty, navigating the airports in her wheelchair. Holly then drove home with her.

I kept seeing her as I had last seen her—slower and more exhausted, but essentially the same person. When I traveled for a visit early in November, I was in for a surprise. She had thin, brittle hair, a sunken-in face, shadow-lined eyes, and she was incredibly slender. I was aware of the situation on some level. However, a change occurs within me during crises. I regain my composure and become quite practical, doing what needs to be done at the time with as much love and kindness as I can. I choose not to process or consider my sentiments at the time. I took care of her and did everything I could to help her feel secure and comfortable without making any admissions about what was taking place.

I still don't understand why I didn't go see her that Thanksgiving, as she requested, given how thrilled I was to be back with her. But I believe it was difficult enough just to see her in that state. I could tell I lacked the power.

I returned to Austin after that early November visit, poured myself into my work, and avoided her a little bit because it was just too difficult to watch her deteriorating in front of my very eyes. She would call and text, and either I would ignore the calls or I would reply briefly via text. She kept asking me to return, but I kept putting it off. I was unable to attend Thanksgiving when she wanted me to. I told her I couldn't go because I had to work, but that was a lie. Everything was untrue.

The Friday Night Lights cast had all met her by this point and had seen her while she was still functioning normally despite using a cane. They occasionally inquired about how she was doing, but I never actually talked to anyone about it. Because talking about something makes it real. I was dodging the subject. likewise avoiding her. Holly, my aunt Sofa, and everyone else around my mother were upset with me for not going. I felt cold. She had always loved Thanksgiving, but on that special day, I was alone in Austin rather than spending the day with her. It was such a callous choice, and I still feel guilty about it.

We boarded separate planes and met in Albuquerque. Dad arranged for a hotel room close by, and Holly gave me a bed in her home. I was almost killed when I finally got to see Mom. Only a few weeks had passed since my last visit, yet she had gotten worse. She was largely absent in her mind, and she didn't recognize me when I walked into her room. Me. I was always everything to her, the reason she got out of bed and kept going. But now, she was clueless about who I was. Although it was amazing, by that point I had mastered the art of downplaying challenging situations. I kept downplaying how serious the situation was and just did what needed to be done.
My responsibility at this time was to look after her. I was there and didn't move till the very end, whether she noticed me or not. I had to concede that this was it after my attempt at denial failed.

As you age, so many of your components gradually disappear. I wanted those brief periods of lucidity to linger forever even though her mind was largely gone. She would then experience brief periods of true confusion. She was still able to speak, but she kept referring to things incorrectly. She claimed that the clock represented a door, the cane a steamer, and the phone a vehicle. She picked up her glasses while watching TV, assuming they were the remote.

I cared for Mom all day and all night. Rick was initially allowed to stay at his hotel, but I persuaded him to accompany me to Holly's home as Mom never left her bedroom. They would never meet. Aside from that, I didn't believe Mom would remember him even if she did see him based on how infrequently she acknowledged me as her cherished daughter.

But she was pretty fidgety today. She had been itching to get up and head to the bedroom window all day. She walked up to the dresser with my assistance and sat there staring out the window. It appeared to me that she wanted to run but was unsure of how to do it. She muttered, "I'm dying," in a rare and fleeting flash of clarity. I felt stunned. She was aware of the situation. What am I to say? What are your thoughts about that? All I could do was tell her the truth. "I realize, Mom, but it's alright. Why don't you join me as I relax and sit down? Not her. She simply remained still longer. "I want to leave the house."

I could not have permitted her to leave the house in this manner. She was only wearing a T-shirt and a diaper, and we would also need to pass Rick in the living room in order to get outside.

"Why don't you just come and lie down?" She pushed me away as I attempted to lead her to the bed. She is five feet eleven and has always been stronger than me; nevertheless, in this moment, fueled by an adrenaline rush, she easily defeated me. I had a battle with her. She continued to strike me while shoving me out of the path. She obviously didn't know who I was. I couldn't allow her to see Rick if she was yelling at me in this manner. She would kill him.
She began yelling at me. Whoever you are, get the fuck out of my way! I'd like to leave. Rick was seated on the couch in the living area when she suddenly burst out of her bedroom. She came to a complete stop when she saw him.

Taking care of her became increasingly challenging over the following few days. She became so unpredictable and aggressive that I was unable to provide for her comfort any more. I was trying to make it so that she could pass away in her own bed. Lucid moments become less frequent. Every time she tried to go asleep, her lungs filled with liquid, and the sound of that liquid rattling around startled her up and worried her. As a result, she was unable to sleep. "What is that?" you ask. We were both surprised and perplexed by it, and neither of us knew what to do. At the time, I had no idea what a death rattle was.

Evidently, she required enough sedatives to kill an elephant. That was the extent of her increased tolerance. Once she was at ease, the procession of people saying goodbye began as she was taken into a room. Holly and Rachel, two of her closest pals, came. Aunt Sofa arrived. Finally, my father David arrived, which caused some tension because Rick was also present. David and I hadn't spoken in years. I didn't want to be in his presence. However, everyone was friendly and set their differences aside. David only lingered briefly. After giving her a forehead kiss and declaring his love for her, he walked away.

The following morning, I climbed into bed with her and surrounded her with my arms and legs. I confessed my love for her to her. The hospice nurse entered the room to check on her as her friends were all seated on the couch inside. He had the kindest bedside demeanor and was extremely gentle and kind. Hospice nurses belong to a unique breed. Actually, angels. They, together with doulas, compassionately lead people into and out of this life.

I stayed in bed with her for hours, observing every breath she took and speculating about which one would be the last. She was now breathing more slowly, and I was unaware of it. Everything came flooding out of me at that very moment. I've just sobbed for twenty-eight years. Never in my life have I ever sobbed so much. I pressed my face into her while clutching on for dear life, not wiping away the tears and snot.

Finally, I stood up, gave her a final goodbye while kissing her gorgeous hands and cheeks.

Rick accompanied me to a funeral home the following day to inquire about having her cremated. That's what she wished for. It became actualized at that point. Days later, I tried to bury myself in sleep and hope that everything was just a horrible dream, but I kept waking up. She had always assured me that everything would turn out OK, but nothing did. She told me as she was passing away that she would leave a treasure trove of keepsakes in her room for me and that I may read the journal she had been keeping for the past few years when she was gone. I wasn't equipped to handle any of that.

My shock at her passing persisted for many years. I had to constantly tell myself that I couldn't call her while having a strong inclination to do so. She left me a voicemail, which I retained and kept listening to. The fact that she had left me a voicemail after I declined her invitation to see her for Thanksgiving made it all the more devastating.

Chapter 19:
Having You Was the Best Thing I Ever Did

When I answered the door at Holly's low-slung stucco house in Albuquerque, where Mom had resided up until nearly the end, David was waiting for me. His expression was dejected and vacant. He walked with a cane and appeared ancient and worn out. The man I had once adored and who had long terrorized me was all but gone. I welcomed him to our small gathering, which Holly and I had organized as a kind of wake in honor of Mom because there wouldn't be a traditional funeral. Mom was always so photogenic, so I'd set up the room with a table displaying lovely pictures of her. I figured we might all want to get together, share memories of her, and find comfort in one another's suffering.

Everything I knew and felt about David seemed to reset as I greeted him. For the first time, I realized that I had never sought his praise; rather, I had revered him out of pure dread. He had long since taught me how to act and to respect him, but I had never looked to David for advice; instead, I had turned to other people's parents or senior friends. David hugged me on the side as he entered the house. I hadn't actually spoken to or seen him since they departed for Boston when I was sixteen until the visit in the hospital. Perhaps there was simply nothing to talk about because there was so much to talk about. But at the time, I didn't understand.

As I prepared a tray of cheeses, I reflected on how much Mom's illness had destroyed me and how, until the very end, I was unable to bear witnessing how the cancer was eroding her day by day. I remained absent in order to keep myself safe. I was a nurse after all, so it was especially weird. Yes, I was a surgical nurse, but I was accustomed to seeing sick individuals of all ages. I could have treated Mom with such love and tenderness if she had been a stranger or a friend.

I had never before found illness repugnant, and nothing can make me feel queasy. In reality, Mom had taken me to visit her father, my grandfather, as he was passing away when I was a young child, around thirteen. Her entire family had remained apart from both of us throughout my lifetime in the hope that she would straighten out and follow their rules if they withheld their love and support. It was customary in her family to experience a lot of suffering and little forgiveness. Mom nevertheless wished to visit her father before his passing in order to be a good daughter. My grandfather was never a particularly kind man. The few times I had visited him as a youngster, he had been cruel to me in addition to being outright abusive to mom. He seemed like an elderly and scary drinker to me, and I didn't feel especially fond of him, but I went with Mom because she valued it.

On the day we went to see him, Dad was unconscious in the dark living room in a hospital bed as Mom said her goodbyes. He began to throw up as she was speaking to him, holding his hand, and expressing her forgiveness to him. He was flat on his back and still unconscious, which was a formula for disaster, but Mom was at a loss for what to do. I rushed to his side as soon as I could and started scooping the vomit out of his mouth to save him from choking to death. Mom stepped back in amazement at how I maintain my composure and knew what to do. When I was a young girl, this man had been cruel to me, and I automatically scooped vomit out of his mouth with my own hands.

But things changed when Mom became ill and started to collapse. I was really worried about her condition. I could have handled it if she had been any other person on the earth, but she wasn't. She was my mother, the one person who had ever been by my side, in any capacity, during my whole existence. She was hurting and decaying, getting smaller and more frailer by the second, as if she were drawn in vanishing ink and dissipating before my eyes, and I couldn't bear to watch. Even towards the end, when I was finally able to be with her before she passed away, I struggled to take care of even the most basic tasks for her, like moistening her mouth with a wet sponge on a small stick. Just not possible for me. Her weakness was difficult to witness.
I had stayed away due to my distaste and numerous grudges, including one against her for not taking better care of herself.

We all gathered in Holly's living room, drinking beverages while lounging on the couch. It was gloomy and dark there. While holding my club soda and shredding the napkin, I waited for someone to speak. I expected someone would volunteer to share a story about Mom's wild antics since I would need a laugh and the opportunity to see things in a more positive light. However, nobody did. Why had I believed that holding this wake would be wise? I was eager for it to be over.

David said nothing at all. If I believed he would face a final judgment, I was mistaken. He showed respect and left quickly. He believed that discomfort should be avoided at all costs. I never again ran into him. He suffered injuries in the fight in the liquor store, and a few years later, he passed away.

There was only one day left for me in Albuquerque. I would finally take the journal Mom had written to me out of the treasure chest Mom had prepared tomorrow. There wouldn't be much left to keep me here after that. or to keep me in any location.

Already, I could see what might be inside. Pictures of the two of us and little love messages. Despite the fact that I don't like charm bracelets, I was confident Mom would have saved at least one particular one for me because she liked them. I was prepared to love and hold onto anything she had left for me. She adored trinkets of all kinds, and I knew there would be plenty there that she had amassed over the years, especially those featuring flamingos. I'm not sure when she decided flamingos were her special animal, but she's always loved them. She still had the same long, thin legs, and when she was cooking, she frequently pulled one of them up and rested her foot against her knee like a flamingo. We got pink birds tattooed on her, including one on her arm with two flamingos forming the shape of a heart with my name inside, and another that covered the outside of her hip and thigh. We also had flamingo lawn statues, little porcelain figurines, and refrigerator magnets all throughout the house. Whatever she had left for me, I knew I would find flamingos among and among them.

After making all the preparations in Albuquerque, I returned to Austin and concentrated on my work. My social life was no longer reliant on the other cast members as I had established my own friendships in Austin. To be honest, the passing of my mother helped put the on-set drama in perspective. I lost the motivation to care what other people thought of me. I had also become better at not taking things too personally. I came to see that we were all merely present, performing our own tasks. I would do my part as well as I could and not regard the actors and crew as the fictitious family I'd hoped they would be. I had at last found a work-life balance that suited me.

That day, I brought Mom's journal with me when I left Albuquerque. She started it when we were estranged, and every entry was addressed to me in the style of a letter, as if she were using it as an opportunity to share her side of the story with me. Since she had placed stickers and stars to every surface of the journal, which had colorful flamingos on the cover (of course!), it reminded me once more that she was truly a child at heart. I had to be careful handling the journal when I first got it from Holly's house unless I wanted all kinds of things to fall out. She had taped in photos, newspaper cuttings, and souvenirs, and the diary was now overflowing with them. The tape caused several of the photos, which I still value today, to be somewhat destroyed. Without realizing the tape would deteriorate over time and thus damage the pictures, she must have thought she was laminating them in place.

While we were apart, she started the journal, and I read about her problems there. As I read it, I developed a picture of her as a complete, lovely, painfully imperfect, and genuinely anguished person who never really got a darn break. She was persuaded by our culture that her value lay in her appearance, and when those features aged and deteriorated, she had nothing left of herself to cling to. She had only me.

I was considering getting a tattoo of her during that time. Although flamingos are really not my thing, I considered drawing a flamingo feather or its outline instead. While reading the notebook, I was struggling to make a decision when I suddenly realized: Aha! That's it. I requested that the tattoo be duplicated and placed on my right arm, just below the elbow. This was logical. It was the ideal way for me to always have her close by.

When I hung off the phone, I wasn't sure I believed her, but the following four hours made me reconsider. On a massive display of socks, flamingos were gazing at me when I entered a store that afternoon. I was walking my dog in the park when I noticed a huge bouquet of flamingo balloons standing behind an energy drink booth. When I got home, I started watching Sex Education, and the protagonist was asking his partner what their safe word would be, only to choose "flamingo." All I could do was smile and think, "Okay, Mom, now you're just showing off," when one of my best friends sent me an Instagram photo that evening showing a group of flamingos lifting off and flying together.

I traveled to Paris for my birthday a few years later. I secretly questioned whether or how my mother might attend my birthday celebration because I didn't think I'd ever see flamingos in Paris. However, as soon as I stepped off the plane and was still in the airport, I noticed a big flamingo mural. The first individual we encountered when entering the restaurant for dinner that night had flamingos all over his button-down shirt. My rosé glass was etched with a flamingo in case that wasn't enough to convince me of her existence. Nobody else in the eatery appeared to be using the same glass. It should be mentioned that this eatery had absolutely nothing to do with flamingos. One could argue that it was a coincidental event at random. But I'm certain it was her.

I can only assume it was for hers. She wished for my affection for her. She desired a partner in her life who would fulfill her and be hers alone. And with or without my permission, I transformed into that person. To be quite honest, there have been times when I've felt angry with her for having given birth to me. All of this was not my request. I never asked for this tragedy or the effort to make enough money to cover the extensive therapy I've required to mend these scars. I did not request these challenging relationships.

Being raised by alcoholic or drug-dependent parents might teach a child to anticipate the needs of those around them. In an unconscious effort to dominate my environment or to feel wanted so that I would feel worthy, I learnt to look out for everyone else's needs and make them happy before I, and it doesn't translate into an honest and genuine connection.

Even if she never made my life any simpler, I still miss my mother a lot and would dearly love and cherish the joy she used to bring. If there's one thing I've discovered, it's how difficult it is to meet someone who radiates such unbridled delight like my mother did. What I miss most about her is her joy. Ironically, the thing that used to irritate me about her is now what I'd give anything for—the twinkle in her eye over the tiniest of things.

I miss having a family member to discuss my mother with occasionally. My friends who have siblings and family who have known them their entire lives inspire me. What must that be like to feel? Yes, one of the best things about my job is that I get to pick my family. My acquaintances who have really problematic families long for the luxury of being able to carefully select their family, like mine. We all have a tendency to long for the things we lack. I have to constantly remind myself to be grateful for the tranquil environment I've built, a place where chaos is not welcome.

Although I attempt to be my own family these days and occasionally feel down, I don't really cry during the holidays any more. I savor the opportunity to either travel alone or with a lover or other pals who aren't seeing their families. A few years ago, my dad and I stopped celebrating the holidays together. He makes me crazy. I've outgrown the idealistic version of him that I made when I was younger and the version that I need him to be. In my adulthood, I have developed my own ideas about who I want to be and see and embrace him for precisely who he is. He espouses fierce love and brutal honesty, for instance. I once believed that was the ideal way to live. But I now think that honesty without kindness can be harsh; these days, I prefer gentle affection.

After my mother passed away, one of the ways I knew to heal the void in my heart was to help other women. I first met Barrett, who is now a dear friend and ally, and his wife Rachel, who had been living in Ethiopia for a year as a result of her social work work there. He informed me when we first met that he had noticed how many women relied on survival sex to take care of themselves and their kids. He enquired as to my availability to assist in finding employment opportunities so they could more sustainably support themselves. Ethiopia has a long-standing custom of weaving on looms, but men predominated as weavers. We made the decision, initially going by the name LiveFashionABLE, "Let's help resource and facilitate a program for women to learn how to make scarves!" (Now called ABLE, it is trying to advance the fashion industry by providing equitable job opportunities for the women who manufacture our products.)

We collaborated with a neighborhood nonprofit that provided six months of rehabilitation to women seeking to quit the commercial sex industry; these women also needed practical instruction if they wanted to learn how to weave scarves. I sat in on a counseling session one morning while I was visiting the ladies in this program, and I observed that the women spoke primarily about the guilt they bore and how they wanted more than anything for their children to never know what job they had done to support themselves. They cried because they were so hurt and humiliated by their pasts. It was at this point that it became crystal evident why I was with them.

Over the years, I've also developed greater empathy for my mother and for myself, as well as a deeper comprehension of the limitations that many women experience as a result of our culture. My mother was a beautiful white woman who enjoyed many privileges, yet she missed out on chances that should have been given to her. She had the chance to enhance her life or fight for her independence, but she chose not to do so because she was unwilling to get past the fears, uncertainties, and anguish that had been passed down to her from her mother and her mother's mother, and so on. So I suppose my task here is to disrupt that trend. Even if it's laborious, someone has to do it. I think that's why I haven't become a mother yet. I'm only beginning to touch the surface of readiness. What an irony. I may have run out of time just as I'm ready to enjoy the pleasure emotionally and mentally. She encountered some of the same obstacles I experienced while attempting to live in a world where males typically have the power. I gained a new appreciation for some of the difficulties she would have had as I overcame my own obstacles to become an empowered adult.

I met Harvey Weinstein at an industry gathering some time after Mom passed away. After our brief conversation, his eyes followed me around the room, so I wasn't shocked when my agent Tracy told me the next day that he wanted to meet with me. The place was designated as his hotel room, but I had a gut feeling that it would not be a good idea to meet him there given the vibe I had gotten from him the previous evening. I must have had the nerve to ask that the meeting be moved to the restaurant and that an assistant be there. I must have had low self-esteem at the time, which convinced me that he couldn't possibly want to meet with me for work-related reasons, but there was something about the slimy way he made me feel the first night that gave me the courage. If I've learnt anything in life, it's to believe my gut when it alerts me to potentially dangerous situations.

But later, when all the #MeToo information out, I understood I had been helping to keep him safe. He asked me not to inform anyone, so he must have known he had behaved improperly. Additionally, I helped him feel better about his offensive proposal by doing so. The only safe course I could see at the time was to claim to be flattered.

I am aware of certain women who graciously accepted the offer. He must have thought the odds were in his favor because he was so confident and nonchalant about it, because there was no way I was the first girl he brought up the subject to. I may have been one of many who answered, "No, thank you." I was merely one of many. Maybe there were even individuals who were bold enough to reject his advances with even greater scorn and disgust. So, I hope.

Women are frequently instructed to reject a man's approaches without ever offending or upsetting him. We've been taught that guys have delicate egos, so if you politely decline his invitation without making a big show of it, you run the danger of making him angry. To avoid injury, we take the necessary precautions. My heart aches for the women and girls who either lacked the experience necessary to go through those situations undamaged or whose objections went unheard.

I thought I had to fight my own issues at the time, therefore I never thought to report him. I didn't believe he needed termination; I didn't even consider it. I reasoned that if I punched him as hard as he hit me, it would make things fair. Albuquerque can be removed from the girl, but not the girl from Albuquerque, I suppose. Although I completely understand that using violence to resolve a disagreement is never a good idea, I made my point at the time and was pleased with how strongly I defended myself. I wouldn't do it this way again.

After that, everyone on the set was aware that such conduct was inappropriate and would not be permitted.

In the twenty-first century, women face pressures like these, and they were considerably more severe when my mother was rearing me in the 1980s. To be clear, even though it's terrible to admit it, we were both extremely privileged women who also happened to be both attractive and white. My mother had numerous chances to organize her life and start making better decisions, but she chose not to.

Additionally, a lot of women, particularly those who are transgender or women of color, must work three, ten, or even twenty times as hard as white cis women yet still not being afforded the same possibilities. In the history of humanity, women have never experienced the benefits of fairness or equality, and this has shaped and continues to influence the paths that are open to us.

Chapter 20:
A Reckoning

Naturally, I was partially to blame for the issue. After dating for a few years, he and I made the decision to start a family. For the first time in my life, I was prepared to pursue this long-held goal. I was overjoyed when we got pregnant. By collecting and implanting the embryo, we put a lot of effort into this pregnancy. My hormone levels were low, so I had to get painful progesterone injections every day, but everything was going great. We prepared the nursery after hearing the baby's heartbeat. I considered the kind of mother I would be and all the things I would provide to this child, whom I had never met. Being the mother of this young boy was the one thing I had ever wanted more in life. Then I miscarried the child. I was devastated.

The familiar patterns that had long confounded me surfaced once more right away. The miscarriage crushed me beyond belief. But because I was in shock on every level—mind, body, and spirit—I downplayed how deeply the loss hurt. Since my partner was at work, I didn't want to bother him with all of my intense emotions or the existential ache that appeared to be ingrained in my very being. My body had suddenly and shockingly failed me, freezing all of our plans and blocking my ability to feel any real feelings. It was simply too much to handle. It was over after a long period of waiting on my part. With IVF, there is reportedly a 10% chance of miscarriage. I suddenly became that statistic, and my strategy for surviving came to the fore.

I've come to understand that I have an incredibly high pain threshold, both physically and emotionally. There have been moments when I have either stayed or returned in disastrous relationships. "Things weren't all that bad," I would say. There's still so much room for improvement. Then, when it didn't work out, I'd blame myself for the breakdown of the relationship and tell myself that if I just improved my behavior and my level of love, I would ultimately experience the same level of love that I was giving. Stupid, gullible girl. This was a flaw in my reasoning. Being accountable and self-aware for one's side of the story is one thing, but far too frequently, I ignored their side of the story and all the warning signs that were right in front of me in an effort to show that I could still make this work. You lack a feeling of self worth that believes you deserve healthy love when you grow up the way I did.

I carried on with my subconscious plan, laughing off what was taking place. Then, I told myself, maybe we could get over this loss without being destroyed by it. I hoped that we would proceed with our future plans.

I had all the same thoughts, but I had no access to my feelings or vulnerabilities. I had given the idea that I cared less than he did by making sure I wasn't a burden to him. I took on the responsibility of making everything ok for him so he could feel better rather than grieving with him. Here it was again—my old, familiar codependent behavior. At all costs, I would put him and his wants ahead of mine, even if he hadn't specifically asked me to.

I've been closely attached to whoever I'm dating throughout my entire career. I've had some amazing relationships and gained so much knowledge from them. Some of those men developed into extremely close friends who are still there in my life now. Some people appeared to merely cause more suffering, while others taught me how trauma appeared to assist me break patterns. But every time, I discovered something new about the areas of myself that required repair. And I don't need to worry if I didn't learn a specific lesson. The same story would apply to the next connection. This recurring pattern highlighted for me where I needed to improve. In the words of Alain de Botton, "We blame our lovers, not our views of love." I've also heard that accepting responsibility is what leads to maturity rather than becoming older. I also came across a quotation that truly spoke to me: "Whatever isn't claimed as our own is projected."

I was alone, and now that I was with my best friends, secure and comforted by their sympathy and kindness, reality was beginning to set in. My barriers broke down and my heart broke into a million tiny pieces since I had no one else to take care of and thus divert my attention by attending to their needs. I had lost everything important to me over the course of three weeks.

The ladies in my life—the one who arrived at my door with a bag and the one with children who couldn't move in with me but would constantly phone and drop off food—were what carried me through that period. the visitors who arrived every other day. They endured my repeated yells at him and breakdowns with the patience of a saint. That would be you, Conor. Khatira. Likewise, Vanessa. Annie. Sandey. Fef. I believed I had lived a good life since I had people who were so devoted to me and who adored me. I'll always remember how these women arrived. I learned about my family because I had so many amazing friends—both old and new—holding space for me.

If I could give the young women who are reading this one bit of advice, it would be to constantly and humbly engage in your friendships with love and intention. Even though I'm not always the best at it, I've finally found a group of ladies that see and get me. They are aware of my heart and are kind to me when I am in need. They've motivated me to support them by being the greatest friend I can be. I appreciate my sisterhood with all of my being because they mean the world to me. The ladies in your lives will always be there, whereas men will come and go.

I had several ketamine treatments following that split. I had nothing to lose. I was forced to face the fact that I was the common factor in all of my relationships and that, if I didn't find a way to heal the young girl inside of me who felt so unworthy of love, my old habits would keep ruining my love life. It became obvious that talk therapy had only helped me so much.

I would take the psychedelic under the supervision of a psychiatrist over the course of eight sessions to see if I could escape the mindset that had held me imprisoned, or at the very least arrive at a different perspective of how I harmed myself in terms of relationships. Childhood trauma is supposedly helped by this kind of therapy, and over time I learned why and how it works so well. I was a scrub nurse, so I was aware of how crucial the anesthesiologist was. The only reason a cancerous tumor removal procedure is conceivable if you have one is because the anesthesiologist discovers a way to get past all of your body's natural defenses. Nobody is going to remain motionless while a surgeon removes a portion of their body voluntarily without administering anaesthetic. We'll all strive to prevent the surgeon from touching our bodies and avoid experiencing that discomfort.

I then realized that the ketamine would act as the anesthetic. It would weaken my natural defenses, allowing me to finally access the sore areas and attempt to treat them. I outlined my aims for the session before ingesting the drug: I was looking for healing of whatever was preventing me from being fully present in my relationships and in my life. I gave the medication thirteen minutes to dissolve under my tongue while the psychiatrist kept an eye on me. This allows the medication to reach my bloodstream sublingually, which is a faster method than simply eating it and letting it enter through the stomach.

I had anticipated that the session would transport me back to my early years, when I had experienced the first trauma and lost my sense of object permanence. where careless parenting led to the development of uneasy attachment. It didn't, though. I was taken back in time to when I was sixteen and living in the small house in Albuquerque that Rudy and I had shared with his father and brother. I imagined that I was watching a movie as I followed Rudy's antics, smelling the shag carpet, hearing his voice, and feeling the panic rising in my chest.

But this was the first time I had ever seen myself from the outside. She was living with a man who didn't want her there as a young teen, doing all the cooking and cleaning alone, trying her best to pull her weight and not ask for anything in return, and yet she had nowhere else to go. Her attempts to obtain the affection and compassion she so desperately desired were continually rebuffed. I spent an hour or more watching this movie of my former life while sobbing bitterly for that girl. I experienced empathy for her that I had never felt before. Such a young woman.

The hour I cried for that little kid was extremely therapeutic, and that new information completely altered everything. That little child is now gradually starting to unwind and have faith in me. She was accustomed to being the one in charge, taking the initiative, and making the plans. But now, finally, I'm attempting to convince her that the grown, adult me is capable of taking charge and making the decisions with the aid of a coach. She can let go at this point because she is no longer required to be in command.

My wish is that she would gradually learn to believe that we are safe, that I am capable of handling situations, and that I am not acting out of panic or fear of being abandoned. She had felt the need to drive the bus for all these years, having to prove her worth to everyone, be likeable, and, by all means, be the one to flee before the person she loved fled from her. However, I am finally in charge of the situation now.

Printed in Great Britain
by Amazon

30331579R00068